COTSWOLD CHURCHES

COTSWOLD CHURCHES

David Verey

B. T. BATSFORD LIMITED
LONDON AND SYDNEY

First published 1976
© David Verey 1976
Printed and bound in Great Britain by
Cox & Wyman Ltd, London, Fakenham and Reading
for the Publishers B. T. Batsford Ltd
4 Fitzhardinge Street, London W1H OAH and
23 Cross Street, Brookvale, N.S.W.2100, Australia
ISBN 0 7134 3054 0

CONTENTS

To the members of the
Gloucester Diocesan Advisory Committee on Faculties
and the Cove of Churches

FOREWORD

In the first part of this book I have tried to consider the architecture of the Cotswold churches in greater depth than hitherto. I have therefore written quite long essays on the Norman and Perpendicular architecture because these are the styles which are prevalent in this district, particularly the Perpendicular. For the post-reformation period I have largely drawn on the Church history of one particular parish to illustrate the trends which were universal in the country.

The second and largest part of the book is devoted to fresh impressions of the churches considered purely aesthetically. I have tried to avoid too many facts because these I have already, in the main, written in *The Buildings of England, Gloucestershire; Vol. I: The Cotswolds*.

I am grateful to my neighbour John Green for his advice to visitors in *The Cotswolds; A New Study*, edited by Charles and Alice Mary Hadfield. 'Know the Cotswolds by its rivers and you will know all,' he says, and I agree sufficiently to have tried to put it into practice in this book; but there are not quite enough rivers.

I would also thank two other neighbours, Canon James Turner whose spoken description of North Cerney Church is written almost verbatim, and Mrs Anne Carver who has herself written so inimitably on the Duntisbournes. I am much indebted to Mr Frederick Sharpe and Miss Mary Bliss for their authoritative and up to date notes on the bells of some of the churches; a unique contribution.

I must also acknowledge my thanks to Mr David McLees who allowed me to read his thesis at the Courtauld Institute on Gloucestershire Churches, and to Mr Alec Clifton-Taylor for his help on many occasions in the past. I am most grateful to Mrs David Langford for her impeccable typing, and Mr Peter Turner for his beautiful photographs; to Mr W. R. Elliott for allowing me to use his unpublished work on chest-tombs, to Miss Sandra Raphael for making the index, to Paul Sandilands and Mr David Stratton Davis for their line-drawings; and to the children of Chedworth (who won the European Architectural Heritage Year competition sponsored by the Woman's Institute for their survey of Chedworth churchyard) for discovering the rare and beautiful iron ledger stone of Thomas Court who died in 1808, and for telling me that, *some of the graves at our church have been put against the wall, because the parsons find it too hard to cut the grass. We think this is a pity, as many of the stones belong to old families. Under the yew tree by the gate there are many graves all belonging to a family called Turk;* finally, and above all, to my wife for encouragement.

I

Introduction
The Cotswolds

THE derivation of the Cotswold is 'Cod's high open land'. The personal name is Old English, and it appears in certain other names in the area, such as Cutsdean, and Codswell, which are in the hills between the head-waters of the rivers Windrush and Dikler; it is possible the same man gave his name to them all.[1]

The name may originally have referred only to the stretch of hill-country between the Cotswold escarpment east of Winchcombe, and the Fosse Way in the neighbourhood of Blockley, Stow-on-the-Wold and Naunton. The word occurs as an affix of Naunton, i.e. Nawnton-super-Cottesold in 1570. 'In recent times the name denotes the whole of this great upland region of Gloucestershire as far south as North-leach, Bibury, Cirencester and Wotton-under-Edge.' This is a quotation from A. H. Smith's volumes on place names, and can be regarded as definitive. Every writer on the Cotswolds however, has had a different idea about where the Cotswolds begin and end. Individuals tend to wish to think they live in them, and are quite insulted if they are told they do not. Robert Henriques, who was both writer and resident, appears to have thought, albeit with some justification, that where he lived was the centre of the district. Ulric Daubeny in the 1920s also kept his limits fairly close. It is the modern authors who try to enlarge them. Having, indubitably, lived in the Cotswolds all my life, I also tend to think of them more narrowly than some. For instance, I hardly think that many of those Warwickshire or Worcestershire places are really Cotswold, any more than are those grand houses with their semi-private churches in 'Beaufortshire' (or is it Avon?). The new Cotswold District Council stretches its tentacles from Chipping Campden to Tetbury and no farther, so in 1974 the question may be regarded as having been settled once and for all; but I dare say I shall go outside the district if I want to, particularly towards Oxford with which the Cotswolds had so many building links in the Middle Ages.

Some church buildings in the Cotswolds have been there for a thousand years. They are the concern of us all, whether we be members of the Church of England or not, for they enshrine our history and our heritage. It is not necessary to have an architectural training to enjoy what has been called 'church-crawling'; but a little knowledge makes it far more interesting, and there are lots of books on the subject these days to help people master the architectural terms which are in general use. What perhaps is even more important is to possess some kind of historical awareness, and a sense of wonder.

Early churches have survived far better than early domestic buildings, and the reason is because most men were still living in mud hovels when they built stone churches on the Cotswolds, for such was the economy in the age of faith. In Gloucestershire alone there survive a hundred Norman churches and scarcely one Norman house. These Norman churches retain Norman features to a lesser or greater degree; but all have been partly altered in later periods.

The changes came about owing to three main causes: firstly structural – the invention of the pointed arch meant that far greater loads could be carried; secondly liturgical – the form of service changed over the centuries, requiring different arrangements such as long or shorter chancels; and thirdly economic; for instance the wool-trade brought prosperity to the Cotswolds and wealth was spent on building and altering churches. There are also historical reasons, such as the Reformation, the Puritans' distrust of images, followed by neglect in the eighteenth century and restoration in the nineteenth. The result is that most churches are a hotch-potch of different styles, and the fascination for the experienced church-crawler is in trying to work out the jig-saw. In order to do this we must recognize the basic styles, Norman, and Gothic comprising Early English, Decorated and Perpendicular. The easiest way to learn them is through the window tracery.

Of course there are other refinements as each period merges into the next, and then there are post-Reformation alterations as well. In addition the church is a store-house of works of art, wood-work, stone carving, painting, stained glass and sculpture, an open history book full of human interest.

Sir John Betjeman, who more than anyone else has been able to communicate to thousands his own personal thrill when opening the door of an unknown church for the first time, told me many years ago that there was no need ever to be dull when writing or speaking about churches. He said if I should write about Kempsford I must not neglect to say that there is an Irish peer buried inside the organ, and it is the only case known to him where such has occurred. The explanation, which the future Poet Laureate did not give, I found out later. At the time of the Regency there was a certain Irish Lord called Coleraine who dealt in coal and went bankrupt, not that either of these achievements were so very wicked; but he feared the devil would get him for his sins. Like other Regency rakes, he preferred therefore, to be buried above ground, and this took place in Kempsford church. When later, they say, there was need for an organ and not much space to put it in, they were obliged to place it on top of and around what remained of Lord Coleraine. There is no notice to this effect in the church; and his epitaph at Driffield states that he was buried there and that he was 'Christian as far as his frail nature did allow him to be so'.

Sir John who has, as everyone knows, a witty turn of phrase, is said to have accused Sir Nikolaus Pevsner of not being able to see the wood for the trees, 'and it's a very big wood', he added. I do not intend in this book to repeat every detail about every church as has already been done in the *Buildings of England*; but rather to look at them more as works of art.

References

1 *Place names of Gloucestershire* by A. H. Smith. Part I, p. 2. Cambridge University Press, 1964.

2
Church Architecture

(i) Saxon

Roman sites produce evidence of the earliest Christians in Britain, and these sites can be excavated; but it is not always easy to excavate the site of an existing church. Until such time as this can be done, most very early church building history must be conjectural. A proper history cannot be discovered simply by looking at buildings. We want to know approximately when a building was built, who were the patrons, who the craftsmen, and the purpose of each part. This degree of knowledge requires written evidence if other dating material is absent, and there is precious little written evidence from the Anglo-Saxon era. From 1066 onwards there are records, and from the thirteenth-century parish records; but Anglo-Saxon is pre-history architecturally. Bede tells about ecclesiastical history, not architecture.

The sequence of a building structure is seeable; but not the date, which can only be proved precisely if written, or by radiocarbon measurements if of wooden construction, or by archaeology. Known dates must therefore be studied with the building. For instance, a grant of land was made to St Aldhelm at Somerford Keynes in 685,[1] which means that the Saxon doorway there could be very early; but exactly how early we do not know. The later sequence of alterations can be looked for on the building, such as straight vertical joints which must mean an addition, and changes of material, and the insertion of features into standing walls. Excavation would, however, show much more, like the different plans of the different churches which have been built one on top of another, possibly right back to the post holes of a wooden church, for many Anglo-Saxon churches must have been built of timber.

The Saxon church at Cirencester, when excavated in 1965, was found to be one of the longest in England. It was under the site of the abbey rather than the parish church, and so opportunity arose for the archaeologists to have a look.

The way to recognize Saxon architecture is by its extreme simplicity of construction, its use of megalithic stones going right through the thickness of a wall at the corner of a building. These through-stones are called 'long and short', which describes the way they are laid, and applies only to this kind of building. Other features, to be found at Coln Rogers, are pilaster strips, stepped footings, and tiny round-headed windows, such features carved from large stones rather than made up of smaller ones. Carved decoration included interlacing circles and pellets, and at Bibury, the capital on the south of the chancel arch is carved with an upright palmate leaf, like the Winchester school of illumination of the late tenth century.[2] The one on the north is in Ringerike style. Many motifs are Scandinavian. Most of the surviving Saxon architecture in the Cotswolds is very late, only just pre-Conquest, and the Saxons had by that time occupied the whole area. The use of herring-bone masonry, that is stones laid like the backbone of a fish, can be both pre- and post-Conquest.

(ii) Norman

About a century before the Conquest, English monasteries had experienced a great revival under leaders like the three saints, Dunstan, Oswald and Ethelwold; however, in spite of the fact that the abbeys continued to hold extensive possessions and to produce notable figures like Aelfric, Abbot of Eynsham, writer of homilies, and St Wulfstan of Worcester, some of the enthusiasm had vanished by 1066 and the number of monks was declining. The monasteries in Normandy, on the other hand, were in their strongest phase of expansion at the time of the Conquest; they were rapidly growing in size and wealth, and few of them were more than 30 years old. They were much influenced by the great Abbey of Cluny, which inspired high standards of liturgical practice and theological study, and they were in contact with centres of learning in other parts of the Continent, unlike the English monasteries which had little inter-communication.

Men of outstanding quality were brought from Normandy to fill high offices in the Church; among the most notable of the new abbots was Serlo of Gloucester. The Norman influence also led to cultural changes; Latin replaced English as the language of devotional works and French ceremonies and chants were adopted. Under Serlo, Gloucester participated in this reform of Church life.

The example of dedicated commitment to the monastic rule as practised at Gloucester encouraged more men to become monks. By 1100, when the Bishop of Worcester granted further lands for the support of the abbey and its new church, Serlo had collected more than 60 monks together, as well as attracting a large number of lay worshippers. It is stated in the abbey's own chronicle that there were

100 monks when he died in 1104, but even if the figure is exaggerated, the abbey was large by the standards of medieval England. It is doubtful whether there was ever much increase at Gloucester after Serlo's time; throughout most of the Middle Ages the number stood at about 50 and in 1534, shortly before the Dissolution, the Abbot and 35 monks acknowledged the supremacy of Henry VIII over the Church of England.

Serlo had already been abbot for 12 years when the foundation stone of his new church was laid by the Bishop of Hereford on 29 June 1089. Why was this not done by the Bishop of Worcester, the saintly Wulfstan? Can it be that the Bishop of Hereford, who came from central France, had something to do with this west of England style employing huge round piers, having perhaps introduced masons from around Tournus? The style seems nearer to St Philibert, Tournus, and the church at Chapaize, than anything in Normandy. It was later followed in a modified form on the Cotswolds; Farmington, with its cylindrical piers and huge scalloped capitals, comes to mind. Anglo-Norman masons, however, produced ribbed vaulting before it was used in France, and Norman sculpture which survives in the Cotswolds was done by native artists, and bears little resemblance to the Burgundian school.

In Gloucestershire all the lay tenants-in-chief were Normans; but Church estates were left largely intact by the conquerors. St Peter's Abbey had benefited, for it held land in 17 manors, together with four manors in other counties. Several of these properties, such as Duntisbourne, had been given since Serlo had become abbot, and the annual value of the abbey's manors had more than doubled. The growth of the Church's wealth was sustained during the remainder of Serlo's long abbacy, and was worthily used by him in the rebuilding of the monastery, which he began three years after the making of the Domesday Survey.[3]

In the Cotswolds the troubles of King Stephen's reign were not unfavourable to the erection of churches. William de Solers built the Chapel of St James at Postlip, so that his tenants might have refuge from the attack of robbers.[4] In return for the tithes the Abbot of Winchcombe undertook to provide de Solers with daily services at Postlip. Architectural evidence shows that many of the Cotswolds churches were built within 100 years of the Norman Conquest.[5] Advowsons of churches were lavishly granted to religious houses.

From 1062–95 Worcester had that splendid bishop, St Wulfstan.

He built many churches in Gloucestershire, and also urged on the lords of the manors the duty of doing so themselves.[6] The Domesday Survey of Gloucestershire had shown that out of a total of about 60 parish churches, 13 were on land belonging to religious houses, the remainder on the property of the Crown or of laymen. The seven Cotswold churches on monastic land were: Bibury, Withington, Stow-on-the-Wold, Bourton-on-the-Water, Broadwell, Upper Swell, and Minchinhampton. The remainder included Coln Rogers, Stanway, Fairford, the Ampneys, Bisley, Driffield, Rodmarton, Lasborough, Lower Guiting, Shipton Oliffe, Temple Guiting, Painswick, Quenington, Stratton, Siddington, Hampnett, Tetbury, Brimpsfield, Southrop, Barrington, South Cerney, Salperton, Syde, and Haselton.

There was certainly plenty of monastic life in the Cotswolds. There had originally been a College of Secular Canons in Cirencester in the mid-ninth century; it was subsequently enlarged, and became Augustinian and under the protection of Henry I in 1117. The new church was dedicated in 1176. By the thirteenth century, Cirencester Abbey was very rich, with great landed property and power in the town. It was also noted for its scholarship in subjects like mathematics and science. Alexander Neckham, whose mother was Richard I's wet nurse, became Abbot of Cirencester in 1213, and has several books to his credit. The stability of his rule, it is said, enabled everyone to work according to his ability. All had to stand when the abbot passed, unless occupied in writing, which indicates the importance he placed on that art. His own writings show observations of natural phenomena, and were more acute than most people's of his day. He observed, for instance, that nightingales sing on the English bank of the Severn, but not on the Welsh.

Most of the Norman sculptural ornament in Cotswold churches dates from after the middle of the twelfth century. A study by Professor Zarnecki of the geographical distribution of beakhead ornament shows that there were two regions where it was particularly popular, Oxfordshire and Yorkshire. Those in Oxfordshire, and the neighbourhood including the Cotswolds, seem to have been influenced by Reading Abbey.

Arches decorated with human, animal or monster heads are a not infrequent feature of Romanesque churches. The heads have been usually referred to in France as *têtes plates;* in England, where an elongated monster head predominates, they are called beakheads.[7] They are more numerous in England than in the rest of Europe. There are said to be 149 monuments enriched with this motif in England. According to Sir Alfred Clapham's definition, the beakhead is 'an ornament taking the form of the head of a bird, beast or monster, the beak or jaw of which appears to grip the moulding across which it is carved'.[8] Human heads can be treated in this way too, with the neck, chin or beard superimposed on the roll-moulding.

Reading Abbey also transmitted the fashions of western France. It was founded by Henry 1 in 1121, and he was buried in front of the high altar early in 1136. The first abbot was a monk from Cluny. It was Henry's favourite abbey on which he spared no expense, and the Empress Matilda, his daughter, also lavished gifts on it. The elements in the decoration of Reading, which derived from Angers, can be linked with Matilda's marriage to Geoffrey the Fair of Anjou in 1128. It must also be said for instance, that the grotesque heads on the west front of Lincoln Cathedral are similar to those at Mesland, near Blois. Political and commercial ties were close in the twelfth century, and artistic links could have been due to Henry of Blois, brother of King Stephen. Those parts of France, so vital as a source for the development of sculpture in England, were also being traversed by numerous English pilgrims on their way to Compostela.

'The doorway at South Cerney is of the Mesland type, decorated with heads and whole animals but no bird heads,' writes Professor Zarnecki. 'A more ambitious work of the South Cerney sculptor is the south doorway at Quenington.' They are in fact very similar; but the latter frames a tympanum of the Coronation of the Virgin. This remarkable subject is the second oldest in existence, the first being the capital carved in Caen stone from Reading Abbey in the Victoria and Albert Museum, *c.* 1130. Quenington is roughly contemporary with Kilpeck in Herefordshire, and is therefore not later than *c.* 1150 During the second half of the twelfth century the Virgin was much venerated.

At Quenington, Zarnecki also sees two beakheads. He then mentions the other two similar doorways both by the same sculptor. The earlier of the two, at Elkstone, shows the imprint of Kilpeck, South Cerney and Quenington and has seven beakheads, and at Siddington, the next work, all but two voussoirs are carved with beakheads.

These examples show the growing popularity of this type of beakhead during the third quarter of the twelfth century, the period to which, with few exceptions, all beakheads belong. The origin of the beakhead is attributed to Viking influence,[9] just as the almond-shaped eyes of the Saxon Deerhurst beast-heads can be seen repeated in many a Norman Cotswold church as hood-mould stops. It seems, therefore, the first impulse came from France, but very soon Anglo-Saxon motifs took over, and were in some cases transmitted back to France. Three other Cotswold churches which have (or had) beakheads, are Windrush, Sherborne and Burford. Windrush has two complete orders of beakheads, the outer over the arch and attached shafts, the inner continuous over the roll moulding and jambs; all are beakheads with almond-shaped eyes, except possibly four or five. At Sherborne there are only the badly weathered beakheads on the jamb shafts of a cottage doorway, all that remains of the Norman church, and at Burford, the west door has some comparatively dull and probably restored beakheads on the roll moulding of the arch.

Beakheads are to be found also on the edge of the Cotswolds in the area roughly between them and Oxford. At Barford St Michael, north east of Chipping Norton, there is a very fine north doorway *c.* 1150, with two orders of roll-moulding overset with beakheads and separated by a band of zigzag. The beakheads continue down the jamb shafts. There do not appear to be any animal or human heads amongst this lot; but at Bloxham near by, where Norman doorways have been re-used in the early fourteenth-century south chancel window arches, there is seemingly a mixture of beakheads and others. At Cassington, very near Oxford, the corbel table goes right round the whole building and there are a few beakheads amongst them; but the most famous example is the other side of the city at Iffley, where the great west door has two orders of beakheads over a roll moulding, and the rosettes on the south doorway and chancel arch derive from Reading Abbey.[10] More elaborately carved doorways on the Cotswold edge are to be found at Cuddesdon, where there are beasts' head stops, Brize Norton, Great Tew, and Enstone, and at Great Rollright there are beakheads. Church Hanborough, which was given by Henry 1 to Reading Abbey in 1121, has a carved tympanum of St Peter, a striking piece of sculpture no doubt carried out locally but inspired by the Romanesque art of Cluny, whence came the first monks of Reading.

Figure sculpture at the end of the first half of the twelfth century, varied considerably in character and quality. In the Cotswolds there is little so explicit as the so-called Herefordshire school of sculpture, which derived from the pilgrimage overland to Santiago de Compostela in Spain of one, Oliver de Merlimond. In the works of this group of sculptors we can detect for the first time since the Norman Conquest, the strong influence of Continental centres on English sculpture, and also the fact that they were executed for lay patrons. These tendencies probably also hold good in the Cotswold area, where figure sculpture is found in Norman tympana. There seems to have been a local exuberance among the English sculptors and masons. The tympana at Quenington, *c.* 1150, have two subjects; one is the Harrowing of Hell, a subject which also appears in Herefordshire, and the other is, as we have observed, perhaps almost the very first instance of the Coronation of the Virgin. At Elkstone, the subject is the familiar Christ in Majesty, seated with Evangelists' emblems and the Agnus Dei, and the Hand of God above, rather unskilfully carved and composed, when compared with the conventional and more sophisticated ornament surrounding it. The Southrop font, *c.* 1180, has greater decorative merit and iconographical skill showing French influence in a more digested form. Armoured women trample on vice. The possible influence of near-by Malmesbury Abbey cannot be overlooked, and its many links with western France. A stone, carved with amphisbaena and foliage, *c.* 1130–40, resembling other springers from the Cloister arcade at Reading Abbey now in the Victoria and Albert Museum, was found at Barnsley, perhaps from a destroyed south doorway, but more likely in some mysterious way from Reading Abbey itself. It is now in the Arlington Mill Museum at Bibury. The sublimest work of the twelfth century is, however, the Head and Foot of a wooden crucifix found at South Cerney, and which, it is now suggested, may in fact be Spanish, and have been brought back from Compostela by a pilgrim. Of local stone sculpture, it most nearly resembles a capital at Leonard Stanley, which is the closest surviving thing in the Cotswold area to the Herefordshire school.

Carved bosses were the innovation of the twelfth century. Romanesque bosses were functional in their decoration. This, Professor Zarnecki says, is admirably expressed at Elkstone, where a boss of *c.* 1180 was given the form of a head with four faces from which the ribs protrude. To increase the impression of security, a belt is fastened across the boss.

(iii) Early English and Decorated

The thirteenth century was a period when the clergy were undergoing a revival of asceticism and were desirous of setting up a more emphatic distinction between themselves and the laity. The consequence was a general rebuilding of chancels, or at any rate lengthening of them, thus creating a new east wall, usually with three lancet windows for the Trinity. What could be more arresting than groups of lancets connected by external and internal arcading and stringcourses? There are examples in the Cotswolds, which was a peaceful and prosperous district then, compared with farther west where serious Border warfare raged. Wyck Rissington and Cherington are two good instances, and it is easy to see how traceried windows developed from their east wall arrangements. Thirty Cotswold churches have Early English features. There are good thirteenth-century chancels at Bibury, Eastleach Turville, Shipton Oliffe, Icomb, Meysey Hampton and Little Rissington.

The Cistercian Abbey of Hailes was founded and endowed with great liberality by Richard Earl of Cornwall, brother to Henry III, in 1246. Not very much has survived; but at the Benedictine Abbey of Gloucester where Henry himself as a boy was crowned King with his mother's bracelet in 1216, there is evidence of a very extensive rebuilding after almost 100 years of stagnation owing to some catastrophic fires.

In 1232 the King, Henry III, granted 100 oaks in the Forest of Dean for work on the abbey and the year following he allowed the abbot to collect dead wood for his mill to melt lead for the roof. The vaulting of the nave, which possibly from poverty had been undertaken by the monks themselves, was finished in 1242. In 1284 John Gamage began his 22-year reign as abbot. Building went on in the different manors, such as the great barn at Frocester, and at Coln St Aldwyns the upper stage of the tower is attributed to this period. The heraldry includes that of the abbey and the de Clares.

At the end of the thirteenth and the beginning of the fourteenth centuries the bishops played an important part in the political and governmental history of England. Most of Gloucestershire was in the diocese of Worcester; but the north-west part belonged to the diocese of Hereford. Bishops were peripatetic magnates, constantly on the move, coming and going, with great entourages and many baggage wagons. Their manor houses on the Cotswolds, therefore, were very convenient for rest and revictualling on their journeys to London from the west. The Bishops of Hereford made frequent journeys to London, and stayed at their moated manor house at Prestbury on their way to their town house in London. One bishop spent Christmas at Prestbury in 1289 and again in 1290. The Bishops of Worcester would stop at their manor house at Blockley. The thirteenth-century bishops were able and energetic, and did much to raise the level of church life, and the lot of the poor, and this continued into the fourteenth century. Bishop William Gainsborough of Worcester, *c.* 1303, was particularly active in visitations and travelled remarkably quickly round his diocese. Bishop Reynolds, 1307–13, excelled in theatrical presentations which appealed to Edward II, who liked nothing better than play acting.[11]

Lay landowners were not numerous. The Clare family, Earls of Gloucester, owned the manor of Tewkesbury and other great properties in the west. The other great landowning family was that of Berkeley, some of whose manors were in the Cotswolds, though, like the de Clares, they were mostly in the vale. The following Cotswold manors belonged to the Berkeley family: Nympsfield, Beverstone, Wotton-under-Edge, Dursley, Westonbirt, Syde, and Uley. Shortage of money was common enough in the Middle Ages. The emptiness of the Berkeley coffers between 1240–60 is in marked contrast to the ease with which they found large sums in the fourteenth century, well before the time when the Black Death had made money more plentiful.

The Berkeleys' steward at Syde, 1334–50, whom we may call William de Syde, had increased responsibilities and powers owing to the lord's absence in the Scottish and French wars, including the nomination of priests serving the many chantries which Lord Berkeley founded, and the education of the lord's sons. In Syde church there is a trefoil-headed fourteenth-century image niche in the splay of a small contemporary north window. Can this be the remains of one of their little chantries?

This same Lord Berkeley, whose magnificent effigy survives in Berkeley church and who in his younger days had only just escaped the accusation of the murder of the King, was responsible for the remodelling of Berkeley Castle, between 1340 and 1350, including the Great Hall with its 'Berkeley arches'. The 'Berkeley arch' is a distinctive feature, found also in Bristol Cathedral. It is polygonal with four or more straight sides enclosing a cusped inner arch with usually slightly ogee-shaped foils. This is the most distinctive thing about what may hopefully be called Berkeley architecture, and it does not unfortunately occur in Cotswold churches. The only feature remotely resembling it is the south doorway at Coberley; but the Berkeleys of Coberley were collateral to the Berkeleys of Berkeley by the fourteenth century, and this curious double archway with its outer order of cusped trefoils may in fact be nearer to the screen between the transepts and the choir ambulatory in Gloucester Cathedral than to anything at Berkeley.

Still clinging to the nomenclature invented in the nineteenth century by Thomas Rickman to describe the Gothic styles, and for want of a better, we must now consider the Decorated style in the Cotswolds, and to tell the truth, there is not much of it, the great periods being Norman and Perpendicular. However, what there is must be doubly precious for its rarity and beauty. Towards the end of the thirteenth century and during the beginning of the fourteenth, up till the Black Death in 1348, Gothic architecture generally reached a pinnacle of perfection.

The chancel of Meysey Hampton was greatly enriched, and has a window of three tiers of trefoils, with a double border of ballflower ornament and a slightly ogee-shaped hood-mould, and the priests' sedilia and piscina have crocketed canopies with cusped cinquefoil arches and pinnacles. Ballflower decoration is not plentiful on the hills; but the delightful little lowside window on the south of the chapel at Coberley has an edging of ballflower. Lowside windows often only had shutters which were opened to allow the sound of the sacring bell to tell the people that the Host was elevated during Mass, and at Coberley, the great manor of the Berkeleys – long since disappeared – was just south of the church, so the window was for them.

At Longborough, there is a fine early fourteenth-century south transept which has a large window with reticulated tracery and pretty buttresses. At Minchinhampton too, the south transept is Decorated, also with a beautiful south window, and supported on the east and west with many buttresses holding up a stone vaulted roof. The little church of Eastleach Martin has beautiful Decorated windows in its north transept, also an addition. In the Vale there is more Decorated work, for instance the ballflower-decorated south aisle of Gloucester Cathedral, and indeed we have to look there for the next change.

References

(I) SAXON

1 H. M. and J. Taylor, *Anglo-Saxon Architecture*, Vol. II, p. 556. 1965.
2 *Buildings of England. Gloucestershire, The Cotswolds*. Note on p. 108. 1970.

(II) NORMAN

3 *Serlo, Abbot of Gloucester*, 1072–1104 by R. H. Harcourt Williams, Gloucestershire Records Office. 1972.
4 *Victoria History of Gloucestershire*, Vol. II, p. 6. 1907.
5 *Ibid.*, p. 7.
6 Wharton, *Vita S. Wulstani.*
7 'Romanesque arches decorated with human and animal heads.' Paper by Françoise Henry and George Zarnecki. 1957.
8 A. W. Clapham, *English Romanesque Architecture after the Conquest*, p. 130 (Oxford 1934).
9 Ruprich Robert, *Architecture Normande*, I, p. 193.
10 *Buildings of England, Oxfordshire*, p. 351.

(III) EARLY ENGLISH AND DECORATED

11 Presidential Address to Bristol and Gloucestershire Archaeological Society by Margaret Sharpe, 1974.

The Perpendicular Style in the Cotswolds

On the Cotswolds, the yields of the wool-trade in the fifteenth century entirely remodelled great churches like Cirencester, Chipping Campden, Northleach, Fairford, Winchcombe, Lechlade, Chedworth, and Burford, and large numbers of churches, in fact nearly all of them, were given new towers – there are at least 40 Perpendicular towers in the Cotswolds – or at least some new windows to let in more light.

By 1327 the great Court masons had progressed to a new style of their own. What we see in the south transept in Gloucester Cathedral is the style of St Stephen's Chapel, Westminster, which had arrived there so to speak, with the body of the murdered King Edward II.

Just before this, Edward's favourite, Despenser, had remodelled Tewkesbury Abbey, as a mausoleum for his family, in the richest Decorated style of the Court, and with the assistance of all that Royal patronage and money could buy. It must have been galling for the Abbot of Gloucester to see his abbey lagging behind and now came his opportunity. The new King built his father's tomb, and gave enough money for the next rebuilding plan of the abbey to be begun, and so the Perpendicular style, England's contribution to Gothic architecture, was launched, and lasted everywhere in England for about 200 years without much change, although there were regional developments; a considerable time lag was due to the Black Death.

The body of the church was the responsibility of the lay people, and wool-merchants were prepared to spend money on it. By contrast, at this date the clergy were generally mean in their expenditure, and as they were responsible for the chancels, these were not usually altered in Perpendicular times. Wool prices reached their highest level in 1480. Rich wool-merchants endowed chantry chapels, soon to be abolished, but not always destroyed, by the Reformation. This was the time when the Cotswolds reached their greatest economic success and international fame and importance, and Edward IV's court favoured a richer architecture.[1]

Even a hundred years earlier the account books of Datini, the famous merchant of Prato, near Florence, show how, in 1382, Datini's organization included the purchase of wool in the Cotswolds. Only two things in Datini's life were important, religion and trade, and on the first page of his ledgers were written the words 'In the name of God and of profit'.[2] His scarlet biretta was dyed in England, and the finest and most expensive wool which he imported was English, and came mostly from the Cotswolds, referred to in Datini's papers as 'Chondisgualdo', and in particular from Northleach (Norleccio), Burford (Boriforte) and Cirencester (Sirisestri).

Here is a typical letter to Datini in Florence, from his Italian agent in London, in 1403. 'You say you have written to Venice to remit us 1,000 ducats with which in the name of God and of profit, you wish us to buy Cotswold wool. With God always before us, we will carry out your bidding, which we have well understood. In the next few days our Neri will ride to the Cotswolds and endeavour to purchase a good store for us, and we will tell you when he has come back.'

At the beginning of the fifteenth century the Papal tax-collectors who purchased wool from the great abbeys, often reserved the amount of the clip they wanted, even before the sheep were shorn. Datini's agent wrote apologizing for some wool from Cirencester which had proved unsatisfactory, by saying he had been obliged to buy up the clip before seeing it, 'For one must buy in advance from all the abbeys, and especially from this one, which is considered the best.' On the other hand, one could wait to buy till the summer fairs, and Datini was told the best time to buy was around St John's Day (June 24) 'for it is then that the Cotswold fairs are held, and that those who want good produce should buy it'. Datini also imported unbleached cloth from the Cotswolds.

By English law, all wool exported for the European market was obliged to go first to Calais, where the Staple was fixed – the only two exceptions included wool for Italy. The Datini records show that the firms he used shipped their wool the whole way by sea, straight from London or Southampton. One of the wool-merchants' brasses in Northleach refers to Thomas Busshe as a merchant of the staple of Calais, and shows the arms of the city of Calais.

It is difficult to imagine how sumptuous the churches were just before the Reformation, with so many chantry chapels fitted up by the wool-merchants. The Garstang chapel in Cirencester is perhaps a good example of what they were like, and there is also a surviving example at Burford; but where for instance was the Wilcox Chapel in Bibury? The abstract of the will of Richard Bagot, 1528, states that he wishes 'to be buried in the Wilcox Chapel in the parish church of Bibury. I give a cow to maintain a taper of 4 lbs of wax to be set before the image of Our Blessed Lady in Wilcox Chapel ... to Oseney Abbey the wages of a priest to sing for my wife's soul and mine for three years in Wilcox Chapel'. All that remains in Bibury church are two nave piscinas, one on the north and one in the south aisle.

The most influential mason-architect in the Cotswolds at the turn of the thirteenth to fourteenth century was, according to John Harvey,[3] Walter, of Harford, a medieval village near Naunton. He worked for the Abbot of Winchcombe, and finished the 'new work'. Winchcombe, of which unfortunately nothing remains whatever, seems to have been more influential than Gloucester at that time; but after the burial of Edward ii it was a different matter. William de Ramsay (iii) was the King's Chief Mason and responsible for Gloucester Castle, and Harvey supposes that a local man called John de Sponlee may have been Ramsay's collaborator in the cathedral. John de Sponlee came from Spoonley near Winchcombe. He then progressed to Windsor where his great work at the castle began in

1350, when he was 'already master mason'.[4] St George's Chapel was started for Edward iv in 1475. Now 500 years later it can be said of St George's that, 'it is the finest example of England's one unique contribution to the visual arts, Perpendicular Gothic. No other building in that style has so flat a vault or such a large proportion of windows to wall. No more light is imaginable'.[5] The lierne vaulting of the nave was not finished till 1509. To what extent were the Cotswold parish churches influenced by this monastic and courtly architecture? There were certainly links with St George's Chapel, as we shall see.

John Harvey has written: 'Probably Gloucester Abbey owes much of its stylistic reputation to the complete destruction of its rivals at Evesham, Winchcombe and Cirencester.' However at Evesham, Abbot Lichfield's early sixteenth-century tower survives as well as his work in the two churches, fan-vaulting and other features similar to contemporary work on the Cotswolds, and farther into Worcestershire at Kidderminster there is an arcade similar to those at Northleach and Campden. All the great religious houses possessed wide-spread manors and churches, and works of importance at these would be carried out by monastic craftsmen. The early Perpendicular of Gloucester choir does not seem to have had very much influence in the Cotswolds where there is a recognizably different type of Perpendicular, and which owing to the time lag is much more akin and nearer in date to the fifteenth century Perpendicular at the west end of the nave at Gloucester, than to the fourteenth-century work in the choir.

The late Professor Geoffrey Webb said that the medieval builder was often required to model his work on some well-known local example, and in consequence features, or whole churches, which appear to have a family resemblance are not necessarily built by the same masons.[6] 'There seems to be a connection between the monumental stonework of the Gloucester tower and, for example, the tower of Chipping Campden, which has the same quality of displayed virtuosity.'

The fashion for fine clerestories was presumably spread by a process of prescribed imitation in the Cotswolds, where the clerestories are distinguished not only for the size of their windows – single, many-lighted windows, not pairs, as in the east of England – but also by their being raised well above the chancel arch, with a window even larger and structurally more daring than those above the main arcades. The result is to produce a lantern-like quality which is very distinctive. It is as though some great college chapel had been dropped into the middle of the parish church. Northleach and Chipping Campden are both good examples of this clerestory treatment; but the handling of the piers and arcades is just as remarkable. In both churches, which are very similar, the piers are octagonal in plan, with exaggeratedly concave sides and extraordinary moulded capitals adapted to this form. The arcades above these piers have notably broad and low four-centred arches. This is a form of arch which is characteristic of the Cotswold area and is usually considered one of the determining motifs, sometimes called 'Tudor', of the final development of Perpendicular in the first half of the sixteenth century. In contrast to the normal medieval pointed arch, the four-centred arch, especially when combined with an almost flat ceiling, introduces an entirely different type of space composition of which the Cotswold churches appear to be 'early examples'.[7] But are they all that early; it would seem from a careful study of the possible dates that they are not.

Dr Joan Evans[8] in describing Chipping Campden, besides also saying that the 'arches of the nave arcade are struck from four centres thus renouncing the true pointed arch which was the basis of Gothic construction', informs us that this was just before 1401, and that the whole scheme was followed at Northleach, and must surely have been by the same master mason. The date 1401 is selected because it is the year William Grevel died, who is described on his brass as the 'flower of the wool-merchants of all England', and it has been supposed he built Chipping Campden church; but of course he did not build it all.

Grevel's will of 1401 shows that he desired to be buried in the church and he left 100 marks (£66) for building. It is true that this sum would buy a large quantity of stone and labour, and it is now suggested that his money provided for work in the north aisle and north chancel chapel. The county historians[9] record a legend in the window over the door of the north aisle asking for prayers for the souls of William Grevel and his wife, and the many mullets, part of his arms, which were dispersed over the windows of the north aisle support this view. The brass of William Grevel and his wife has been moved, and it was probably situated on top of a tomb-chest – like the Tames' one at Fairford – and would have been placed where he was buried in that part of the church which owed its existence to him, 'perhaps the north aisle or chapel temporarily monopolized for performance of the rites directed under his will, whereby four chaplains were to celebrate daily for ten years'.[10]

The transformation of the fifteenth century at Campden started *c.* 1450 and finished with the nave arcades, clerestory and tower at the end of the century.[11] Grevel's money may have provided a building fund after expenditure on his tomb and chapel; but for the main expense later in the century we must look at the will of William Bradway,[12] dated 6 June and proved 1 July 1488. The abstracts include, 'To the building of the nave and body of the church 100 marks.' This is as much as Grevel gave, and it clearly states that it is for work in the nave. Other wool-merchants in the fifteenth century have left brasses, like William Welley, who died in 1450 but whose will is not known. Two of the three main forms of tracery in the church are dateable to before 1488. The date of 1460 for work on the south is based on the sculptured label stop of a woman's head-dress similar to that in the Prelatte brass at Cirencester, *c.* 1462. The problem for the builders in 1488 was that of inserting a new nave with arcades between two existing aisles, an existing chancel, and to allow for the tower on a restricted site to the west. This was exactly the same problem as there had been at Northleach.

John Fortey died in 1458, and his will desired that he should be buried in Northleach Church in the 'new middle aisle', and he gave £300 to carry on and complete work 'already begun by me'. Fortey was paying to have the nave finished. Could this nave and the one at Campden be by the same master mason? The Northleach nave would antedate Campden by 30 years according to this, though work could have been in progress at Campden when Bradway died. Is it likely a master mason would use a plan 30 years after he first used it? Something like this must have happened. The nave arcade mouldings, bases, capitals and soffits are similar. Elevationally too, they are the same with five tall arcades resting on octagonal piers with exaggeratedly concave sides, producing the distinctive capital. Above the arches are recessed clerestory windows with strip pilasters rising from the capitals to surround the windows. Although the clerestory tracery of the two churches is different, there are not enough differences generally to suggest that a new master mason was involved, and 30 years is not after all an unreasonable working-life span for a mason. There is nothing quite like these two arcades anywhere near, except at St Mary's Kidderminster, and Rock, and at Church Hanborough

"Northleach . . . as though some great college chapel has been dropped into the middle of the parish church."

in Oxfordshire on a smaller scale, and at St Helen's Church, Abingdon. At Abingdon there are not only the nave arcades, north and south, with the same concave moulding carried up into the capitals, and four-centred arches, but also there are additional arcades either side treated in exactly the same way. In the Cotswolds, however, there is also the arcade at Rendcomb, which is presumably copied from Northleach.

The builders of Winchcombe were more economical than they were at Northleach and Campden; for instance, the piers are octagonal but they did not go to the expense of fluting them. Henry VI was somewhat precariously on the throne when Abbot William of Winchcombe began to build a parish church. The abbot of course, made the chancel, and the rest was built by the parishioners, helped by Sir Ralph Boteler of near-by Sudeley Castle, before his disgrace in 1469.

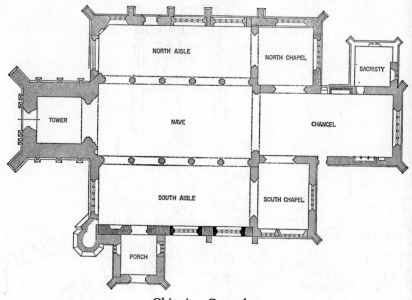

Chipping Campden

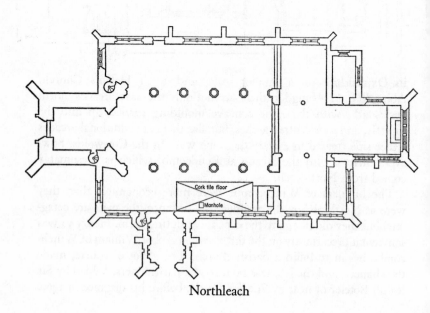

Northleach

In this case there is no structural division between nave and chancel. The abbot's dates are 1454–74. Some of the tracery in the aisles can possibly be related to Northleach (a possession of Gloucester Abbey), and some to the west front of Gloucester, which dates from 1421–37. There are diagonal buttresses on the tower and east end, free use of crocketed and ogeed pinnacles, and continuous battlements with mitred mouldings, all found often on the Cotswolds besides at Northleach and Campden. The Winchcombe clerestory however, is set in the plain wall, not divided by vertical mouldings as it is at Northleach and Campden, and the tracery is square headed, causing strain on the central mullion. Building their church cost the lay parishioners of Winchcombe, £200.

Fairford also can be classed as a complete rebuild except that the position of the central tower was retained. It was paid for by the merchant John Tame, and was built during the last quarter of the fifteenth century. The feeling of unity is enhanced by the complete set of contemporary stained-glass windows, now famous throughout the world. Most of the architectural detail shows great refinement, particularly the bowtell mouldings. The bowtell is a small round moulding, or bead; also the word is used for the shafts of clustered pillars on window and door jambs, and on mullions.

At Cirencester, the story is more like Northleach and Campden with another inserted nave; but there is also a far greater degree of lateral expansion, and the tower came before the nave. The tower was begun soon after 1400, directly after the rebellion of the Hollands, half-brothers of Richard II, against Henry Bolingbroke, when Thomas Holland, Earl of Kent, and the Earl of Salisbury, were taken by the townspeople of Cirencester and beheaded. Henry IV was obviously pleased with the Cirencester folk and his arms (France ancient changed to France modern, *c.* 1406) appear, or once appeared according to Bigland, on the west front of the tower.[18] The west window tracery is like the south-west window at Gloucester (1421–37). The Trinity Chapel at Cirencester must be *c.* 1430 because of the use of the Duke of York's badge, the falcon and fetterlock, and Richard Dixton's will, 1438. Dixton and Prelatte were members of the weavers' guild of the Holy Trinity. Almost at the same time the Garstang family chapel was formed on the south, and the tracery of the windows on the south is similar to the four in the Trinity Chapel on the north.

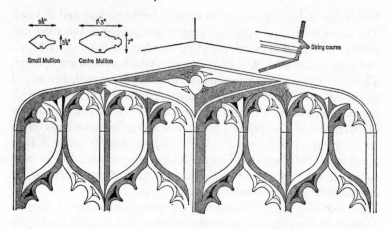

The Lady Chapel cannot be much after 1458. However, the really big Perpendicular alteration was the insertion of the nave and that was altogether later, and financed by the tradesmen of the town. The will of a butcher called John Pratt in 1513 left £40 for work to begin within one year on the middle aisle. Leland, who visited Cirencester between 1535 and 1543, describes the church as ' . . . very fair. The body of the paroch chirch is all new work, to which Ruthal, Bishop of Duresme, born and brought up in Cirencester, promised much, but preventid with deth gave nothing. One Alice Aveling, aunt to Bishop Ruthal by the mother side, gave an hundred marks to the building of the right goodly porch of the paroch chirch'.

The nave, which has a pierced parapet with sculptures on the stringcourse resembling St George's Chapel, Windsor, rises many feet above its thirteenth-century predecessor with an almost continuous clerestory row of four-light windows including a great window over the chancel arch. The arcade piers are very tall, compound, with eight thin shafts. The arch below the clerestory is panelled. On each side of every pier are shields born by demi-angels, carrying the arms or merchants' marks of the contributors. As late as 1532 a merchant left £20 for the completion of the rood screen.

This is getting very near the end of Cirencester Abbey, which was dissolved in 1539. It is astonishing how unaware some of England's abbots were of the gathering storm. If they had not been, how could they have indulged in such conspicuous display as they often did? The last abbot's monogram, which must be 1522 or after, appears on the external keystone of the east window of the nave of the parish church, whilst his predecessor Abbot Hakebourne's is over a pier capital, showing the progress in building. Hakebourne's mitre and initials also appear in the fan-vault of St Catherine's Chapel, with the date 1508. This may be similar to destroyed cloisters in the abbey; but it seems impossible to think that it is part of them, reset at the time of the Dissolution, as has been suggested by some writers, not, however, by Bigland, who says Bishop Ruthal paid for it. Henry VIII's injunction that the abbey should be totally destroyed would in any case, preclude such a work of conservation.

I have now described what happened to the four or five most splendid Perpendicular or 'wool' churches in the Cotswolds during the fifteenth century; but similar alterations took place to a lesser degree in almost all the smaller parish churches.

At Bibury the nave was heightened and given an almost flat ceiling and clerestory with two-light straight-headed windows under an embattled parapet. It appears also that Oseney Abbey must have provided the chancel with a Perpendicular roof, but that went in the nineteenth-century restoration. One window, that on the west end of the south clerestory, has ogee lights with many cusps, and the great west window of the nave is not unlike the west window of the Trinity Chapel at Cirencester. If then, these alterations are mid-fifteenth century, the lay donors' names are unknown. The late fifteenth-century wills at Bibury do not appear to give moneys for church building other than for chantries.

At Chedworth, the south wall of the nave was rebuilt with a magnificent series of very typically Cotswold Perpendicular windows by one, Richard Sely, who was either a wool-merchant or the Nevilles' bailiff, about the time of the Battle of Bosworth, 1485.

At Withington the tracery of the big east and west windows resembles the work of Abbot Morwent's time at St Peter's Abbey, Gloucester: full-blown Perpendicular with the horizontal transom element in the central top light. The upper stage of the tower is extremely elegant, with its large bell opening having four trefoil-headed compartments surmounted by six small traceried lights under an ogee-shaped and crocketed hood-mould. The buttresses are not diagonal as is usual in the Cotswolds, but straight and panelled. The battlements have tall panelled pinnacles with pretty finials rising from winged gargoyles at the corners. The lord of the manor was the Bishop of Worcester.

The majority of churches were given Perpendicular towers; but Withington is specially elegant, so are the towers at Hawling and Coates. Again, the Hawling tower does not have diagonal buttresses, but they are at right angles overrun by a continuous stringcourse. Ogee-headed bell openings, battlements, pinnacles, gargoyles, they are all on an elegant small scale, the work of an exceptional master mason.

Of the 41 Perpendicular towers in the Cotswolds, 33 have diagonal buttresses and 8 do not. The tower at Coates appears also to be fifteenth century, with the more usual diagonal buttresses, but all refined and delicate.

Nowhere in the Gloucestershire Cotswolds are there ambitious Perpendicular alterations comparable to the naves of Northleach, Chipping Campden, and Cirencester; however, there is Chipping Norton, which could by a stretch be considered to be a Cotswold place in Oxfordshire, and its circumstances are similar, in that it underwent a complete remodelling from the profits of the wool trade. The nave of Chipping Norton, c. 1485, must therefore rank with other Cotswold churches which had naves inserted into existing buildings. It has piers with clustered shafts which continue upwards unbroken by capitals to support the now modern roof. They are the only divisions between the windows of the continuous straight-headed clerestory. The wall below has a panelled grid with cusped arches that continue the pattern of the tracery, and large quatrefoils in the spandrels of the pointed arches of the arcade. There is the familiar east window over the chancel arch. This is said to have been paid for by a wool-merchant called Asshefylde, and it certainly achieved the desired lantern-like effect.

If we followed the river Evenlode on its course from the Cotswolds, just before it joins the Thames near Oxford, we should find the most beautiful and unspoiled church of St Peter and St Paul, Church Hanborough. The advowson belonged to Reading Abbey and the manor was part of the royal manor of Woodstock. In the fifteenth century there was considerable building activity at two or more periods. The tower and spire must be quite early in the century and were evidently inserted in the west end of the nave.[14] The arcades and clerestory must be later as there is visual evidence of an earlier roof line over the east tower arch. It has been suggested[15] that the alterations were possibly of 1399, when a Papal indulgence was granted to contributors to the church fabric; but this ought not to be regarded as putting the nave so early in view of the fact that the tower came first. Therefore for the nave we have an unknown date in the fifteenth century. The extraordinary thing is that these arcades so closely resemble those at Northleach and Campden, except that the arches are more pointed. Here are the same elegant octagonal piers with exaggerated concave mouldings which are repeated and emphasized by the capitals. Miss Sherwood[16] says this is a type common in the Cotswolds; but I know of no others except at Northleach, Campden, and Rendcomb. Can this be the work of the Northleach master mason? The ashlar came from Taynton, near Burford.

The neighbouring church at Eynsham is almost in the same case, and indeed could well be, but there are other possible prototypes in the Oxford colleges, in the antechapels at New College, All Souls and Magdalen. It received a new nave *c.* 1450,[17] or later, with octagonal piers with concave mouldings having extra concave pilasters either side, so that the whole pier is usually described as oval or oblong in section, and this is similar to the Oxford colleges. The capitals follow the concave mouldings, and are strikingly like those at Northleach and Campden in spirit.

This treatment of capitals is a usual Perpendicular mannerism but generally on the bowtells of an even more composite pier, and therefore smaller in size and clustered together. Indeed this is what the mason of the Oxford Divinity School, Richard Winchcombe, did there and elsewhere, notably in the Wilcote Chapel at North Leigh, another border-line Cotswold place in Oxfordshire. River communication between the Cotswold quarries at Barrington, Taynton and Burford, and these Oxfordshire places was possible for the movement of stone, and the river Windrush was used for this purpose. Once it had reached the Thames, of course, it could be sent on to Windsor and London.

In trying to assess by eye the influence of the Perpendicular architecture of St Peter's Abbey, Gloucester, on the Cotswold churches, we are driven to the conclusion that it did not happen much before *c.* 1400. The first Perpendicular window at Gloucester is dated 1335, and there followed the transformation of the choir which has pointed Gothic windows in the clerestory, with Perpendicular tracery. The panelled walls have arches divided in the middle and this feature does occur in some Cotswold churches, usually with less success; but the later four-centred arches are not to be found here. The cloister, *c.* 1377, also has pointed two-centred arches and panelled walls, and of course, the first fan-vaults.

The alterations of Abbot Morwent, who had it in mind to rebuild the nave and started at the west end some time between 1421 and 1437, are, however, very much copied in the Cotswolds, particularly the windows on the south-west corner with their four-centred arched heads, vertical mullions running through the sub-arches (this occurred in the windows of New College Chapel, Oxford in 1379), and bowtells on the jambs with little bases and capitals, though in this case they are never concave. The great west window has a four-centred arched head, and tracery which seems familiar on the Cotswolds, and flying buttresses (cf. Chipping Campden). The west doorway has a neat bowtell frame, hollow moulding, and carved spandrels, the prototype of many. The south porch, which is of this date or earlier, seems very like the early fifteenth-century porch at Northleach, with its vault and bosses, and panelled walls having only the central lights glazed and therefore treated differently on the exterior. The Gloucester porch is much restored, but the south doorway has its original concave mouldings, and bowtells with bases and caps. Northleach was a possession of Gloucester Abbey, and the interiors of these two porches create much the same artistic feeling.

The great tower was built in the 1450's and is covered in canopy work with arches flatter than most in the cathedral, but hardly to be called four-centred. There is a great transom band of quatrefoils, and the splendid open-work parapet and pinnacles are, of course, far more elaborate and expensive than most things attempted on the hills. The Lady Chapel was built *c.* 1450–99, and the windows have pointed arches and come into the grid category, which is not a usual feature of the great Cotswold churches, although there are sub-arches in the tracery pierced by verticals as in the first Perpendicular window a century before. They are very tall windows with no less than four layers of transoms all with varying tracery.

The finest small-scale Perpendicular work is in the little Chapel of the Salutation of Mary, and this is refined in almost the same kind of way that Richard Winchcombe's work was refined.

The Bristol or Berkeley influence on Gloucester, in the flat many-cusped arches of the ambulatory screen, is not often found in the Cotswolds, though there are exceptions in the south doorways at Coberley and Newington Bagpath.

R. H. C. Davis's study of mason's 'banker' marks in Oxfordshire and the Cotswolds[18] throws an interesting light on to the problems of dating, and development of a local style of Perpendicular architecture in the Cotswolds.

The marks emphasize that, although most of the greater Perpendicular churches so far from being finished in one generation may not have been completed within a century, the greatest individual period of building in Oxfordshire and the Cotswolds was *c.* 1440–80. For an example of the long building period there is Cirencester, with its tower of *c.* 1402, and its nave arcades of *c.* 1514–36. Winchcombe alone was built all at once. 'This is a commentary both on the state of order in the land during the Wars of the Roses, and on the state of the wool-trade. For not only is it clear that while the land was not sufficiently disordered to make church-building impossible, the political uncertainties of the age prompted such safe investments as the Church and stone and mortar, and it also seems that the abnormal state of the wool-trade encouraged building. For in this period, the wool-trade experienced a number of most amazingly acute but short slumps and booms; one year a woolman might have been poor, in the next he would have had more than enough to build.[19]

The great Perpendicular churches were built by first-class masons, whose marks are elaborate many of them have 'pedigrees' or 'parent marks'. They were the personal trade-marks of individual masons. It seems they were usually used when many masons were being employed on a building as a check against faulty workmanship. When a mason wanted to perpetuate the mark of his father or master, he adopted it with a 'difference', usually adding an extra line or curve. For instance, a mason's mark at Kempsford is found at South Leigh and at Northleach with added differences, another at Chipping Norton appears the same, and with a difference in Northleach nave. This may mean that the same mason (and his son or pupil) worked at Chipping Norton and on Northleach nave. The same relationships can be deduced between Church Hanborough nave and Northleach porch. There are other theories, however, which hold that differences denote qualifications or proficiency. Freemasons read many secret meanings into lines and numbers.

Gargoyles were as popular with the masons in the fifteenth century as grotesques had been with the Normans. Unlettered masons probably had a system of symbolism in their carvings which slyly mocked their employers, thus preventing the sin of covetousness. Once finished, these great new churches were the marvel of the neighbourhood and small details were copied by the village crafts-men in their own churches. Such eccentricities of design as the crown of the tracery of the east window of Northleach chancel are found repeated in the neighbouring churches of Turkdean, Aston Blank, and Coln Rogers. Similar masons' marks are not found here; it was just a case of copying.

The more skilled masons moved around, and it is obviously impor-tant for the purpose of dating, to know the average working life of a fifteenth-century mason. One cannot expect it to have been more than 30 years, so that if a mark can be dated by documentary or other evidence, the same mason's mark elsewhere provides a most useful date bracket.

The heyday of the Cotswold churches did not last long. By the beginning of the sixteenth century the number of new works is de-creasing and the supply of masons falling. The marks show that the 'Cotswolds school' was just as closely connected with Oxford as with Gloucester. None of the marks in the Lady Chapel of Gloucester Cathedral, finished *c.* 1500, have been found elsewhere, nor does it resemble the Cotswold churches. The earlier west end of the cathedral, as I have already indicated is a different matter.

A mason working in 1383 on New College Chapel, Oxford (founded by William of Wykeham in 1379), also makes his mark on Northleach porch, for which there is no documentary evidence, but the costume portrayed in the carvings is very early fifteenth century. The ante-chapels of New College, Magdalen and All Souls have apparently stylistic influence in the Cotswolds. Another mason whose mark appears on the Northleach porch, makes it again at the Wilcote Chapel, North Leigh, begun in 1438 to the designs of the master mason Richard Winchcombe, who died about that time. The North-leach porch, as we have already seen, resembles in style the great south porch of Gloucester Cathedral, dated *c.* 1420. The panelled walls have certain lights glazed but not all, and some arch forms are very pointed.

Another mason, whose mark looks like a simple loop, flourished in the last half of the fifteenth century. His mark appears on the south nave aisle wall at Northleach before 1489, on the Burford nave arcades in the mid-late fifteenth century, at Minster Lovell before 1485, at St George's Chapel, Windsor, on the north wall of the nave, 1475–83, and at Oxford Cathedral Cloister a year or two before 1499. The occurrence of his mark at Windsor is not surprising, since masons were impressed from all parts of the country to work there, and because much Taynton stone was used in the building of the chapel.

There is a legend that John of Gaunt, who died in 1399, built the the tower at Kempsford but this is documentarily groundless and chronologically improbable. A more interesting tradition is held by the family of Couling, that its ancestor was a mason brought from Oxford to build the tower. This tradition corroborates the mason's mark at Magdalen College, Oxford (founded in 1458), which may, according to the Magdalen Register, have belonged to one, John Colas, who worked on the chapel. This was between 1474 and 1479; but before this, the mark appears at Burford, on the south porch and north chancel aisle, at Stanton Harcourt in the exquisite Harcourt aisle *c*. 1471, and in Pope's Tower, and in the marvellously beautiful church at South Leigh. The Bear and the Ragged Staff in the porch at Burford suggests that it was built by the Nevilles who held the manor 1439–99. A similarity between the design of the work at Stanton Harcourt and Kempsford has been observed. The use of single-light rectangular windows in Pope's Tower is reminiscent of the lower stages of the tower at Kempsford.

The next mark to be noticed by R. H. C. Davis is a cross + on top of a W, $\frac{+}{W}$ found between 1430 and 1461. It appears on the Trinity Chapel at Cirencester *c*. 1430–38, at Sudeley Castle *c*. 1450, on the church tower at Kempsford and at Winchcombe Church 1454–61.

We now come to the most exciting connection of all as it is the one most obviously expected from stylistic grounds, that between Northleach and Chipping Campden. It is a St Andrew's cross, joined on three sides but open at the top, IXI. This mark has not been found elsewhere except at Chipping Norton. The dating of the two similar naves has already been discussed, and the connection with Chipping Norton is corroborated by another mason's mark; however, the nave arcades at the latter are quite different and have composite piers, and the clerestory looks almost like a wall of glass, the windows having straight heads and grid tracery with only narrow divisions between them.

Another mark on the Northleach nave arcades, *c*. 1458, appears at Winchcombe, at Fairford, and on the lower portion of Cricklade church tower. At Fairford we must, therefore, presume a date prior to *c*. 1488. All the churches in this group belong to the Cotswold type of Perpendicular. The work is characterized by its four-centred arches, deeply hollow casement mouldings, neat detail and elaborate and varied tracery, in contrast to the broad details and gridiron tracery of much Perpendicular elsewhere.

At Northleach on the south-east column of the nave arcade there is the graffito of Henrie Winchcombe, and on the other side the words 'God grant us his grace' and 'Edmunde'. It has been supposed that Henrie Winchcombe could have been the master mason or quarryman; but this supposition may be groundless and there have been Winchcombes in the district for many years since. Merton College in 1448–50 bought Taynton stone from one John Wynchecombe of Windrush.[20] Richard Winchcombe died about 1440. He was the master mason employed at the building of the chancel of Adderbury between 1408 and 1418,[21] for New College, Oxford. In 1413–14 he visited Taynton to obtain stone, his travelling expenses being charged in the accounts. The whole family might have originated in the Windrush/Taynton quarrying area.

Mason's marks do not provide any direct evidence for the identity of the master mason of a building. The master mason, *lathamus*, was both the medieval architect and the chief of the working masons, at one and the same time. It was he who supplied such designs as were used, and who supervised the actual work of building. There is little to be found in medieval archives about plans or drawings. The master mason supplied patterns for mouldings and other details; but much work must have been done by eye alone, with plan or elevation.

The master mason, however, does appear to have attained almost professional status. He is frequently called 'Magister', not in the academic sense, but as a title of honour. He had special privileges such as a gown of livery, a house or lodging, various special allowances and above all, he took and trained apprentices. His importance will be realized when it is remembered that practically every problem of building was a masonry problem, and that in the absence of textbooks all necessary knowledge was acquired by practical work at the bench. Powerful and brilliant men like William of Wykeham were no doubt great builders in that they originated and financed great works of building, but they were not architects.[22]

We know quite a lot about the master mason Richard Winchcombe, because of the survival of the detailed accounts of the building of the chancel of Adderbury, Oxfordshire, 1408–18. He was there in each of these years except in 1411, and was in fact the 'architect'. It may well be that the authorities of New College, satisfied with the work done for them at Adderbury, recommended him to the notice of the university. By 1430 he was in complete charge of the building of the Divinity School, which he had designed. There are the most striking likenesses between Adderbury and the Divinity School. Both works are remarkable for the subtlety and delicacy of their mouldings. The bowtells are specially slender, and in both buildings they are provided with little bases of a most refined section. At Adderbury these bowtells do not have capitals. The great east window has five ogee-headed lights and fitting tracery under a four-centred arch with hollow moulding, and a castellated transom. The doorways have quatrefoils in the spandrels and hood-moulds with deep stops. There are buttresses with pinnacles, below the parapet level and triangular shaped, with little ogee gables, winged gargoyles on the parapet, and in several places sculptured heads of William of Wykeham, who was actually dead before the building began. On the north of the chancel is a vestry with an oriel window, all part of Winchcombe's design, which has a neat bowtell surround, tracery over the ogee-headed lights, and battlements on the parapet. This distinctive Perpendicular style of Richard Winchcombe found just on the Oxfordshire side of the Cotswolds, occurs also at Deddington, Broughton, Bloxham, and of course, in the Wilcote Chapel at North Leigh. We can in this case, associate a series of medieval buildings with a master mason whose name we know. He not only designed his buildings, but he also built them, as a true architect should, and as apparently it was the custom to do, until the architects of the Renaissance preferred to leave the actual construction to others.

F. E. Howard considered the Gloucester school of mason-craft was the most skilful in vault design and construction in the early part of the fifteenth century. 'Nobody could have designed the vault at the Divinity School who was not conversant with the vaulting of Gloucester Cathedral'. Winchcombe seems to have preferred the four-centred arch to the two-centred one usual at the time, and this, and his trick of treating the top and bottom of tracery lights with a similar pointed and trefoiled arch, fitting neatly into the cinque-foiled ogee arches of the main lights, is found in many Cotswold windows. Winchcombe's style is generally more delicate and refined than for instance the Perpendicular to be found at Canterbury or even the Winchester School of the period, which is marked by boldness of scale and largeness of detail.

Before the murder of Edward II, Tewkesbury Abbey had been

refurbished in the Decorated style of the Court by Despenser. Winchcombe Abbey also may well have had similar treatment. Did not Joan, daughter of Edward I and married to a de Clare, give birth to her son at Winchcombe? The Perpendicular remodelling of Gloucester, however, must have put this abbey ahead of the others in its fashionable influence, and from this point the Perpendicular style spread throughout England. There is a considerable time lag before the peak of Cotswold Perpendicular building, well on into the fifteenth century; but what had developed during this time at Winchcombe Abbey or Cirencester Abbey is still an unanswered question.

In the work of this known master mason called Richard Winchcombe, and in default of any other, we can see an influence spreading right across the Cotswolds, in the early part of the century, just before the great Cotswold Perpendicular churches were built, an influence which may well have affected the anonymous master masons of many subsequent buildings in between Gloucester and Oxford, as they pressed their daring innovations in obtaining more light to the very brink of structural failure.

References

THE PERPENDICULAR STYLE IN THE COTSWOLDS

1   *The Cotswolds – a New Study*, 1973, p. 238.
2   Iris Origo *The Merchant of Prato*, 1957.
3   John Harvey, p. 13. *English Medieval Architects. A Biographical Dictionary down to 1550*
4   *Ibid.*
5   Philip Howard, *The Times*. 1975.
6   Geoffrey Webb, '*Architecture in Britain in the Middle Ages.*' Pelican History of Art.
7   *Ibid.*, p. 180 and 183.
8   Dr Joan Evans, *The Oxford History of English Art*. 1307–1461. 1949.
9   S. Rudder, *New History of Gloucestershire*, 1779.
10 P. Rushen, *History and Antiquities of Chipping Campden.*
11 David Verey, *Buildings of England: Gloucestershire. Vol. 1*, p. 153. 1970.
12 P. Rushen, *History and Antiquities of Chipping Campden*, p. 25.
13 R. Bigland, *History of Gloucestershire*, Vol. I, p. 347. 1791.
14 E. T. Long. *The Story of the Parish Church of Hanborough* 1972.
15 J. Sherwood, *Buildings of England: Oxfordshire* (1974), p. 544.
16 *Ibid.*, p. 360.
17 *Ibid.*, p. 600.
18 Oxfordshire Archaeological Society Report 1938. No. 84.
19 *Ibid.*

20 J. E. Thorold Rogers, ed., Oxford City Documents. Oxford Historical
Society, XVIII, 1891, p. 323.
21 John Harvey, *English Medieval Architects.*
22 'Ricardus Wynchecombe, Lathamus' in the Oxfordshire Record Society
Series, Vol. VIII.

(a) *Pulpits.* There were not many pulpits before the fifteenth century.
However, the wooden pulpits at Evenoled and Stanton are said by
Crossley and Howard to be late fourteenth century.[1] They also say
that when pulpits became general in the fifteenth century, probably
only a quarter of the churches were in fact provided with them, and
they then add that any county with more than ten examples is for-
tunate. There are Perpendicular stone pulpits on the Cotswolds at
Ampney Crucis, Chedworth, Colesbourne, Cowley, Cirencester,
Naunton, North Cerney, Northleach, Turkdean, Lasborough, and
Winson, so this easily puts Gloucestershire into the fortunate category.
There are Jacobean wooden pulpits in several places, such as Oddington St Nicholas, Shipton Sollers, and Windrush.

Nineteenth-century restorers usually found the pulpit fixed against
the first pier west of the screen, sometimes in the north side, sometimes in the south. Ecclesiological theory however, often caused them
to move the pulpit a bay farther east so that it was either one side or
other of the chancel arch, preferably on the north or gospel side.
Stone pulpits of course, are more often found *in situ*, as they are more
difficult to move than wooden ones. The Cirencester pulpit is in the
traditional position against the first pier on the north side of the
nave.

References

1 *English Church Woodwork 1250–1550.* Second Edition, p. 275. By F. E.
Howard and F. H. Crossley.

(b) *Screens.* 'The Midland type of screen with vertical tracery
panels was sometimes affected by East Anglian influence; at Fairford and Cirencester ogee arches are applied to the tracery of the
narrow bays usual in those districts.'[1] At the Reformation, the chantries were suppressed and their endowments confiscated, but while
the guild chapels were thrown open to the church by the destruction
of their screens, the heirs of the founder of a private chantry chapel
usually insisted on their rights to the fabric, and used the chapel as

a private pew. On this account a number of beautiful examples have survived, such as those at Burford and Cirencester. Occasionally a tomb is arranged to come directly under a screen, and the latter is arched over it. This occurs in work of the early sixteenth century over the Tame tomb at Fairford.

A great deal of devotion was paid to the rood in the Middle Ages; a hanging lamp was generally suspended in front of it, maintained perpetually at Burford. At festivals, multitudes of tapers, usually placed on the rood beam, were lighted in its honour. This led to an almost complete destruction of roods at the Reformation. In Gloucestershire, Bishop Hooper (afterwards to be burnt at the stake by Queen Mary Tudor) ordered the destruction of rood screens as well. This is probably the reason why so very few have survived. Woodwork anyway was never the *forte* of Cotswold builders as it was in East Anglia and there are no roofs comparable with many in Norfolk and Suffolk.

References

1   *English Church Woodwork* by F. E. Howard and F. H. Crossley

(c) *Porches.*   There is a group of Cotswold churches with porches which have niches in their east walls, the purpose of which has long been a subject for speculation. It is quite a distinctive feature which does not often occur elsewhere, is always of late medieval date, and individually of different shape and design.

Among the many churches which have them are the three Ampneys – Crucis, St Mary and St Peter – Aldsworth, Barnsley, Bibury, Winson, Little Barrington, Baunton, the two at Eastleach, St Martin and Turville, Westwell, Notgrove, Salperton, and Haselton. The damaged remains of a Crucifixion which may have stood in the niche survives at Coberley, and at Great Rissington reset in the porch is a late fifteenth-century carved stone panel with a shallow canopy and embattled cornice of which the upper half has the Crucifixion.

At Aldsworth where the porch is on the north (usually they are on the south) the niche is late Perpendicular, like the rest, but it has a pierced stone cresset to hold candles and a narrow flue for the smoke. The niche is also fitted for a grille and for doors. Is it a poor man's chantry? At Barnsley, which belonged to the same group of churches as Aldsworth, coming under Bibury, it is also the north porch which survives and the niche is also rebated for a door. The stone seats survive in the south porch at Ampney Crucis. At Ampney St Mary, the niche is partly made out of an incised twelfth-century grave slab; at Ampney St Peter the niche is now in the vestry, and it is of the same shallow type as at the other Ampneys. The Haselton niche has a cinquefoil head and a floor or sill which contains part of an early sepulchral slab with an elaborately incised cross, and the Salperton one has a crocketed ogee arch.

M. D. Anderson in *History and Imagery in British Churches*[1] says that to a medieval community the porch was almost as important a focal point in their lives as the church itself. When Chaucer said of the Wife of Bath 'husband at the church door had she five', he meant what he said. A marriage contract was made in the porch before the couple went in to celebrate the nuptial mass. Church porches therefore sometimes contained an altar at which contracts could be sworn, and this would of course have been on the east wall, with perhaps a niche behind to contain an image. Stone benches were often placed along the walls of the porch and there is a known case, not in the Cotswolds,* where the bench on the east wall is raised in the centre to form an altar table.

We really do not quite know to what extent the porch was used for other purposes. It is still an official respository for secular notices of local government. In the fourteenth century upper storeys were often added, which culminated in the fifteenth-century porches like the one at Northleach, pinnacled, embattled and 'image-ridden'. At Cirencester, the great south porch was built in *c.* 1490, apparently by the abbey but with lay money on land belonging to it, probably for its secular business with the Royal Commissioners on financial matters, increasingly sent round by the Kings. After the Dissolution it was known as the Town Hall. A stone dole table for bread distribution was introduced into the ground floor in the seventeenth century.

* South Pool, Devonshire.

References

1 M. D. Anderson, *History and Imagery in British Churches*. John Murray, 1971.

(v) Post-Reformation

Post-Reformation churches, or church alterations, hardly exist in the Cotswolds before the reign of Queen Anne. There was, however, a great deal of alteration to church furnishings. Jacobean pulpits abound. Archbishop Laud introduced altar rails. Fonts went out with Cromwell and came back with Charles II.

The famous spire at Painswick was rebuilt in 1632, and with the coming of the eighteenth century several towers had to be completely rebuilt, and they may usually be considered examples of Gothic survival rather than revival. Dursley tower was rebuilt in 1709, Somerford Keynes in 1713, and Blockley in 1727. The only eighteenth-century classical tower is that at Bourton-on-the-Water, 1784. The nave and south transept at Sapperton are classical and rebuilt in the time of Queen Anne. The north aisle of Chalford was built in 1724, and the south aisle at Painswick in 1741; but the latter has not survived. The wonderful collection of seventeenth- and eighteenth-century table tombs in Painswick churchyard is typical of many smaller churchyards in the Cotswolds, and is unequalled anywhere. Inside the church there is a carved stone reredos by John Bryan, 1743, alas, now hidden behind the organ. The church at Hawling was mostly rebuilt in Georgian classical *c.* 1764, and there is still a Georgian chancel arch at Didbrook. At Temple Guiting there are Georgian windows inside Perpendicular surrounds, and a classical Venetian window in the transept. It was usually difficult for Georgian innovations to survive Victorian restorations, just as it has been hard for some Victorian things to survive the age of the 'ghastly good taste' of the twentieth century.

The reasons for the almost wholesale Victorian restorations were partly because of neglect to the fabric during Georgian times and partly, of course, due to the Oxford Movement, and revival of religious fervour. It is said that Holy Communion had been celebrated so seldom, people began to forget its meaning. The church-warden would raise the chalice to the curate. 'Your very good health, Sir.' 'The very good health of our Lord Jesus Christ', replied the curate. Spit was used instead of water and when the sermon began, a lunch-tray was carried into the Squire's box-pew, which was often fitted out like a room with a fire-place. As early as 1673, when the vicar of Bibury preached for two hours, turning the hour-glass that stood on the pulpit, the squire would withdraw, smoke his pipe, and return for the benediction.

Post-Reformation ecclesiastical history, for instance in Bibury, shows that nearly all the incumbents were long lived, and having found such a delectable place to live in they were reluctant to leave it. There seem to have been only about ten vicars in 300 years. One of the first, however, was disreputable. In 1563, Richard Bagge was accused of not saying Divine Service every Sunday and of committing adultery with his servant. After 1641 Benjamin Winnington did 32 years; John Vannam, who married the widow of Squire Richard Sackville, 1673–1721; Thomas Baker, ancestor of the Lloyd-Baker family, 35 years; William Somerville 1756–1803; Charles Coxwell for only a few years (although Rector of Barnsley from 1767 till 1829). His daughter married the Squire Richard Cresswell, whose brother Sackville Cresswell was vicar from 1809–43.

The holding of livings in plurality must have been quite profitable, if curates could be found to carry out the few duties absolutely necessary. Parsons also lived very well off tithes in kind. The Rev. Thomas Baker, vicar of Bibury, wrote in 1729: 'Lent tithes which are collected are as follows: for every cock, three eggs; for every hen, two eggs; for every duck, two eggs: and for every calf weaned, a halfpenny: for every calf sold, four pence or the left shoulder: if one sow has seven pigs, one tithe pig is paid. Tithes of turnips sold were taken in kind by my servants, and tithes of walnuts were paid by Mr. Coxwell.' In the same year Mr Baker was able to buy 67 acres of land in the parish of Shorncote, presumably as an investment, which it proved to be for his descendants.

Charles Coxwell was born at Ablington Manor in 1740 in the house built by his ancestor in the reign of Elizabeth 1, and which still stands on the banks of the Coln. He got an exhibition at Pembroke, Oxford, from the grammar school at Northleach. His elder brother died of the smallpox, so at the age of 22 Charles was Lord of the Manor, and the following year he was ordained. His family were not wealthy, but the estate was entailed and it was now his; even so he became curate of Cote in Oxfordshire, curate at Chedworth, Compton Abdale, and at Bibury, and when he was 26, rector of Barnsley, which office he held for 63 years. His marriage to Mary Small of Cirencester lasted for 60 years and produced 13 children. At one time he also held the rectory of Coberley during the minority of the intended incumbent, and he only went there once in four years, for which he was paid over £500. He also held the living of Marston Meysey, a poor one, for 35 years, and he left no record of ever visiting it. He eventually resigned on the grounds that he was 'unwilling longer to retain the cure of souls whom he could not benefit by his doctrine'. He actually resided in Barnsley from 1771–83. In 1787 back at Ablington, as a magistrate he heard minor cases in his own house. Poachers were fined £5 and their goods seized for payment. Rectory land at Barnsley was let for droves of Welsh cattle making their way to London for the market. In 1789 he had the livings of Badgeworth and Shurdington, which he visited eight times in 17 years, and his interest seems to have been almost wholly financial. Of course he had a curate, but he had livings of his own and the churches seem to have been very badly served. As he grew older his duties increased and he became Deputy Lieutenant of the County, Rural Dean of Fairford and Chaplain to the Bishop of Bristol. He held the living of Bibury, as we have seen for three years, while waiting for his daughter's young brother-in-law, Sackville Cresswell, to take Holy Orders. To do this, he had to resign Badgeworth and Shurdington; but he must have thought it worthwhile as the income from the living of Bibury was at least £1,000 a year.

This seems to be an extreme, though perhaps not unusual, case of pluralism. To be fair, it must be said that Coxwell had to have a licence from the bishop to live at Ablington instead of at Barnsley Rectory, and this had to be renewed at regular intervals.

By the standards of those days, Charles Coxwell was a good man. In contrast to the indifference in which he held his more distant livings, he had great interest in his parishioners near his home. Two cottages at Barnsley he let free as a parish house, for the poor. He started a dame school for the village children to be taught to read. He employed several women over the years, but Elizabeth Keen, first employed in 1768, was to continue until her death in 1828. At Bibury he spent £20 a year on sheep to be divided amongst the inhabitants of Bibury, Arlington, Ablington and Winson 'soon after Christmas', and here he also paid for children to be taught to read, and bought their books. Of himself, he wrote that he 'was never fond of cards . . . but chose rather when he could be excused to dedicate his evening hours to reading and the improvement of his mind. Being but a timid rider, he declined the exercise of hunting; but was fond of shooting, albeit he was a very indifferent marksman as being near-sighted and obliged to make use of glasses. He had some knowledge of music and performed but poorly on the violin, having never had the benefit of any regular instruction nor opportunities for playing in concert through his residence in a country village. In his department as a magistrate, he was accessible to all and gave the meanest complainant a patient hearing. In every case which would admit it, he inclined to mercy and never signed but with reluctance a warrant of commitment to prison. And lastly from the time when he ceased through bodily infirmity to preach his sermons in church, he derived a pleasure from perusing them in his study. . . .' He died in 1829.

(vi) Restoration and the Oxford Movement

> *The moon above, the church below*
> *A wondrous race they run,*
> *But all their radiance, all their glow*
> *Each borrows of its Sun.*

JOHN KEBLE

John Keble, author of *The Christian Year*, a Victorian best-seller, and the most influential leader of the Oxford Movement, was born in 1792 in Keble House, Fairford. This was his home for 43 years. He then became vicar of Hursley until his death in 1866. Keble College, Oxford, was built in memory of him. The presence of such a man, writing such a book, and living in their midst, must have had a great influence on the Cotswold clergy. There was also his brother Tom, who was vicar of Bisley, and who almost ran a 'school' for high church curates. Nearly all Tom's parishioners were weavers engaged in the Stroud cloth industry. To them a bad harvest could mean starvation, and so Anglo–Catholicism here had to be associated with the cause of the workers.

Tom Keble employed as architect to build Bussage Church J. P. Harrison, who was reputed to be 'of no great note in his profession, but an Oxford man, a gentleman and a scholar'.[1] However, according to another account he was 'the leading light of the Oxford Architectural Society and a follower of Pugin and Carpenter'.[2] Bussage was financed by subscriptions from Oxford undergraduates with Tractarian leanings. That was in 1846. The restoration of Barnsley church had begun in 1843, but Harrison was only called in there by

Canon G. E. Howman after J. M. Derrick's engagements elsewhere became pressing, so the two works are probably contemporaneous.[3] Derrick was the architect employed by Pusey at this time, to build St Saviour's Church in Leeds, in the very worst of that city's slums, where the clergy adopted a ritualistic type of worship which appealed to their poor parishioners. In the Gloucester diocese there was a High Church curate at Tetbury who afterwards became the famous Father Lowder of London Docks, who managed in 1848 to build St Saviour's, Tetbury, a little church for the poor, but perfectly Tractarian with a sanctuary by the great Pugin himself and the rest by Samuel Daukes.

In 1847 Harrison was asked by Howman to design a chapel of ease at St Michael's Burstow. Howman's father was vicar of Shiplake till his death the next year. In the first letter, written from No. 11 Chancery Lane, Harrison says: '. . . before I say yes or no to your kind proposal I must ask what are the old fashioned arrangements to which you allude, for I perhaps may have still older ones which I should not be able to yield.'[4] Thus the clergy and architects were egging each other on in the revival of medievalism. Harrison goes on to say that a church at Burstow will cost £300 or £400 more than the same building would be in Gloucestershire, and other things about the relative costs of Decorated or Lancet windows. Mr Howman appears to have been a little impatient, and Harrison reminds him that as he has just restored Barnsley Church he must realize how busy he, Harrison, is, with three or four jobs on at the same time. 'I never intended to promise that the designs would be ready much before the spring, but only a plan and pencil sketch to show to Mr. Howman senior . . . I have to design a church, I believe, for Ridley of Hambledon before I can do much for Burstow.' What became of these projects is unimportant compared with his work for John Keble at Hursley in Hampshire, where at this very moment (1846–48) he was building a church, lych gate, schools, and schoolmasters' house.

The church cost £6,000 and was built from the royalties of *The Christian Year* and Keble's second collection *Lyra Innocentium*, published specially for the purpose. The style chosen was Decorated, unlike the lancets he used at Barnsley; but Harrison seems now to have thought a bigger window saved money on the cost of solid walling, and in any case the Gothic revival had more or less settled on middle pointed as the most correct form. Harrison managed a spire too, whereas at Barnsley there had been insufficient money, and luckily for us the little Elizabethan or Jacobean tower was left. The Hursley spire has not survived.

The interior layout of Hursley was based closely on Neale's and Webb's 1843 edition of Durandus' *On the Symbolism of Churches and Church Ornaments*, the bible of ecclesiology. The windows are by Wailes to a scheme based on the medieval windows at Fairford. The west window of 1858 was redesigned by Butterfield. At Barnsley the windows which are not by Willement are by Wailes, and Butterfield designed the plate and altar ornaments, or perhaps the design was simply taken by the maker Keith, in 1854, from one of the pattern books, like *Instrumenta Ecclesiastica*, published by the Ecclesiological Society, formerly the Cambridge Camden Society, and illustrated by Butterfield.

Father Lowder at Tetbury in 1848 had ordered from the great firm of John Hardman, of Birmingham, a set of church plate designed by Pugin. Another curate, the Rev. Edgar Edmund Estcourt of Cirencester, was also busy in 1845 obtaining Pugin-designed plate from Hardman.

Before Keble went to Hursley he was taking a keen interest in the Gothic revival in the neighbouring churches round Fairford. There was time off from sowing the seeds of the Oxford Movement in Southrop Vicarage (where he was curate), when Hurrell Froude came to stay. Architecture was one of Froude's many hobbies. The two friends both disapproved of flat ceilings and round or square-headed windows which were the rural fashion. 'We are in hopes to counteract the taste of the churchwardens who seem to have unenlightened views of pure Gothic,' Froude wrote to his father. Froude was really the only leader of the Oxford Movement to be deeply interested in architecture. Keble, Pusey and Newman cared much less about the ecclesiological side of church-building, although Keble should have been fascinated by the curious symbolism which the Victorians learnt from the medieval writer Durandus, by way of the Ecclesiological Society. Regeneration was symbolized by octagonal fonts, the atonement by a cruciform plan and gable crosses, a hood-mould over all three lancets meant the unity of the Trinity. Keble wanted people to worship in a church in which the services could be conducted in a decent, orderly and reverent manner, and he wished that church to express the unity of the Church of England with the Catholic Church throughout all ages. Kneeling, for instance, was to be encouraged, and so he must have approved of Butterfield who designed pews in which it was far more comfortable to kneel than to sit.

Meanwhile Tom Keble had discovered the architect G. F. Bodley, and needing yet another church for the mill people in the Stroud Valley, he commissioned a new church at France Lynch. This was only Bodley's second church, almost his first, and he had not yet, in 1855–57, met the pre-Raphaelites; that was to come the year following. The church is architecturally interesting, being a break away from the usual Gothic revival to something more French. It was also thoroughly in tune with current liturgical thought; the effect of elevation given to the altar by six steps is remarkable. The polychromy and marble inlay of the sanctuary and the use of lapis lazuli and malachite in the low choir screen, pulpit and altar retable are very sensitive. Bodley had previously added an aisle at Bussage, and was later to build Selsey Church, this time with the added attraction of having the pre-Raphaelites to do the windows.

References

1 Georgina Battiscombe, *John Keble*, 1963.
2 Nikolaus Pevsner and David Lloyd, *The Buildings of England. Hampshire*
3 Trans. B.G.A.S., Vol. 76, 1957, page 178.
4 Unpublished letters from James Park Harrison to the Canon George Ernest Howman in possession of Colonel Little.

(vii) Cotswold Churchyards

The Cotswolds can be divided as regards the distribution of elaborate churchyard tombs into east and west sectors by drawing a line between Cirencester and Winchcombe.[1] All flamboyant seventeenth- and eighteenth-century tombs are in the West. 'Bale' tombs are an eastern feature.

Table-tombs, perhaps better described as chest-tombs, owe their origin to tombs inside churches which resemble long boxes providing bases for recumbent effigies. A large number of late seventeenth and early eighteenth-century ones are as wide as they are high and twice as long thus forming the popular 'double cube'. Early seventeenth-century tombs are more slender. Chest-tombs have capping stones, either a ledger stone, or a lid like a casket. 'Tea-caddies', a Painswick name, can be concave-sided, octagonal or cylindrical. Lids are more usual in the east sector.

The earliest chest-tombs (*c.* 1611 onwards) are often close to the porch, with heavy ledgers, sharply cut backwards underneath, surmounting a body which is narrower and lower than later tombs. Lindley[2] says 'Inscriptions are cut with a strong sense of pattern which is the basis of good lettering; as with early Roman inscriptions there is little if any space between words'. Some have arched panels on the ends or an arcade of them on the sides. Tombs with arched panels are found in a cluster of places in the east Cotswolds, Buckland, Snowshill, Evenlode, Oddington, and Daylesford. The largest collection of these 'primitive' tombs occurs at Broadwell. There is a fine double tomb, with a typical inscription, at Snowshill. They continue to be used after the end of the seventeenth century. There is an abiding taste for simple dignity, and there is a difference in approach between the tomb which is basically simple but with slight ornament, and the joyous, triumphant exuberance of the lavishly decorated tombs.

Lyre-shaped ends. These are tombs with ends which project on each side, curving outwards towards the bottom, like a lyre in shape. These become frequent as the seventeenth century develops and continue well into the eighteenth. The motif may come from the gables of Dutch houses, and may have come to England with Nicholas Stone who arrived from Amsterdam in 1613. It was used for every purpose of ornamentation, on fire-places, doorways, and mural tablets. The lyre shape is a console ending in a coil resembling the volute of the Ionic capital, a typical feature of Renaissance architecture. Once given the idea of the lyre-shaped ends the masons treated them in many delightful and elaborate ways, such as the leaves of the acanthus to form a decoration like the Composite order. The acanthus leaves on the sides of the consoles turn outwards and fold back inwards halfway up the curve; cherub-heads, skulls, hourglasses, fruit, and flowers cling to the sides.

Particular varieties of lyre consoles appear in clusters, of greater density in west Gloucestershire in the villages where the clothiers lived. They are rarer in the east; one at Stanton, Temple Guiting, and Sevenhampton, two at Chedworth, and one at Quenington, the only one combining both lyre and bale.

End panels can be treated in other elaborate ways, framed in wreaths of flowers or emblazoned shields. Four tombs have portrait busts, at Bourton-on-the-Water, Daglingworth, Harescombe, and Leighterton. There are also the symbols of death, hour-glasses, the bearded face of Father Time, skulls (sometimes bat-winged), cross-bones, inverted torches, drapes and the occasional urn. In contrast there are serpents biting their tails to indicate eternity, cockle shells for life's pilgrimage, palms of victory and trumpets of triumph. Winged cherub-heads signify souls winging their way to heaven. At Elkstone two girls are comfortably seated, each on a large skull which has been placed on a stand to give it the right height. The finest of the Restoration tombs are clearly the creation of masons who revelled in their skills and in the stone which gave them full scope for their artistry.

Tea-caddies. Tea-caddies seem to find their natural setting in Painswick churchyard, but they also appear on the Cotswolds at Leighterton, Minchinhampton, Miserden, Nympsfield, Owlpen, Ozleworth, Pitchcombe, Salperton, Siddington, Uley, and Withington; and at other places below the escarpment where indeed many of the best churchyards like Upton St Leonards, Elmore, and Standish are situated. Few can be confidently ascribed to Painswick masons, though ones at Dowdeswell, Sevenhampton, and Hawling may derive from Painswick. There is a typical Painswick tea-caddy at Salperton dated 1779, while inside Salperton Church is a wall monument, dated 1782 and signed by J. and J. Bryan.

'Bale' Tombs. These tombs are capped with a large semi-cylindrical stone which covers most of the ledger. Nearly half of these capping-stones are scored with deep grooves, running either laterally over the curved top or diagonally across it, hence the tradition that they are meant to represent corded bales of cloth and be connected with clothiers. This cannot be, because they are situated on the east of the Cotswolds and not in the clothiers' stronghold on the west. Another theory connects them with the law that shrouds should be made of wool, and another with the hearse which was often placed over a coffin when it was being carried into the church. The banded bales look quite like a hearse, and the addition of finials may represent the candle sockets of the hearse. There is also the chest in the church with its rounded lid and reinforcing hoops, as a prototype. The area where

they are found is small enough to suggest that only a few masons' workshops were involved, and it is interesting that the tomb at Fairford of Valentine Strong, the famous mason from Barrington and Taynton, is a bale tomb, and dated 1662. It could be that this was a fashion emanating from Strong's yard. The tomb of Kempster, the other great mason of the period, is also decorated with a bale at Burford. Burford is the centre of the bale tomb area, and they can be seen at Fulbrook, Swinbrook, Asthall (with finials), Westwell, Little Barrington, Windrush, Broadwell, Bourton-on-the-Water, Stow-on-the-Wold, Lower Slaughter, Wyck Rissington, Yanworth, Bibury, Eastleach, Meysey Hampton, Poulton, and Southrop.

Generally all but the finest tombs are the work of local masons operating over a restricted area.

Apart from the Painswick tea-caddies of the Bryans, very few tombs can be ascribed to a particular mason. We know that Edward Woodward who died in 1766, made the Woodward family tomb in Chipping Campden churchyard. There is a chest tomb at Ampney St Mary signed by Tempany of Arlington, Bibury, and one at Minchinhampton dated 1761 signed by the local mason Iles. Some names appear on inside tablets and also on brass plates attached to churchyard tombs. Tempany and Iles also appear on brass plates; but they are later than the great period of Renaissance tombs.

References

1 W. R. Elliott. Chest-tombs by Cotswold and Severn. Unpublished manuscript.
2 K. Lindley. *Of graves and epitaphs*. Hutchinson, 1965.

3

Cotswold Churches
as Works of Art

Visitors have been advised to know the Cotswolds by its
rivers. Of these the Churn, the Coln, the Leach, the
Windrush, and the Evenlode are the most important, but
they have many tributaries within their own private valleys
like the Ampney Brook, the Dunt, the Eye and the Dikler.

In the east the Cotswolds slope imperceptibly into the
basin of the Thames, and all the rivers flow east to swell the
Thames, except those in the Stroud valleys, like the Frome
and Aven which flow west into the Severn.

The Cotswold churches are, therefore, described in
relation to the rivers, and are grouped geographically,
rather than as in an alphabetical gazetteer; there is, however, an index on page 195.

THE CHURN VALLEY

Coberley, Cowley, Colesbourne, Rendcomb, North Cerney,
Bagendon, Baunton, Cirencester, Watermoor, Preston,
Siddington, South Cerney, Stratton

The Churn is one of the reputed sources of the Thames, and the point where it rises at Seven Springs is, in fact, the most distant source from London. It is only four miles here from Cheltenham, which lies under the Cotswolds in the Severn vale. Between its source and Cirencester, the Churn runs through some great private estates, which were, anyway in the nineteenth century and with a few obvious exceptions, incomparably grander than elsewhere in the Cotswolds. The first four we come to, Coberley, Cowley, Coles-bourne, and Rendcomb, all have churches more or less in the private grounds of the big house, although the circumstances of each are now quite different. The great house at Coberley disappeared in the late eighteenth century. The mansion at Cowley is now a conference place owned by the County Council. Colesbourne is still private with a house rebuilt on a smaller scale, and Rendcomb is a public school.

COBERLEY

The church is approached through a barn and the garden of a farm-house. To the east and south of the churchyard is a great wall with Renaissance openings on the far side now blocked, which are all that remain of the great house of the Berkeleys, and later the Brydges, Chandos, and Castlemain families. The north side of the church looks, and is, rebuilt. This occurred in 1869–72 and John Middleton was the architect. We have to go round and find the south porch to enter. On this side there are several interesting features connected with the south chapel and porch.

The chapel was built as a chantry, *c.* 1340, by the Berkeleys. There is a low-side window with an edging of ballflower and a hood-mould with large head-stops. It is quatrefoil in shape and had a wooden door which used to be opened for the ringing of the sanctus bell at the raising of the host during the Mass. This could then be heard in the big house. There are also three quatrefoil windows on the west side of the porch. The doorway has a flat outer arch with prominent cusps not unlike the archways on the screens of the ambulatory in Gloucester Cathedral, with a moulded four-centred arch behind.

The Perpendicular tower has diagonal buttresses on the west, battlements and gargoyles. There is a large sundial on the south stair turret dated 1693. The west window is of the grid-pattern type.

Middleton's detailing of the nave appears fussy with too much extraneous carving. However, there are some old stone carvings, a fifteenth-century crucifixion, and also in the sanctuary, a small bust of a knight – a heart burial – *c.* 1295. In the chapel there are the effigies of a Berkeley knight and his lady, second quarter of the fourteenth century, and a young man with widely curled hair, only slightly later.

A ring of three bells; one by Messrs. Warner, 1870; another by Edward Neale, 1661; and the tenor, a remarkably fine bell from the Worcester foundry, 1410, inscribed in Gothic majuscules: AVE MARIA GRACIA PLENA with the 'Royal Heads Stamps' of King Edward III and Queen Philippa as word stops.

COWLEY

Set in the landscaped grounds of Cowley Manor, a mid-nineteenth century classical mansion, the church is a small building of *c.* 1200 with a Perpendicular top stage to the tower. This top stage is elegant, and was even more so before the pinnacles were broken off the battlements. The belfry openings have four-centred arched heads with ogee crocketed hood-moulds and three ogee-headed lights. There are panelled pilasters at the corners – not diagonal – and these are slightly boxed out on the string-course, a subtle refinement, not usually met with on the Cotswolds, giving a distinctive silhouette like some Somerset towers on a smaller scale.

Otherwise the church has single lancet windows throughout, and little change from nave to chancel. Inside it has a comfortably religious atmosphere, with a gold mosaic reredos, and close-fitting carpet, suitable as a retreat from the conferences next door.

The churchyard has one specially delightful table tomb with a man and girl in contemporary eighteenth-century clothes in life, and opposite, their souls in heavenly garb.

Henry Brett, the noted campanologist, who became Master of the Ancient Society of College Youths (of London) in 1701, lived at Cowley Manor. He gave three of the existing bells in 1697. They are by Abraham Rudhall 1, who also cast another in 1707. The tenor is by John Rudhall, 1812;[1] the treble by Mears, 1857.

References

1 The foundry of Rudhall's was situated in Gloucester circa 1694–1845.

Left (1) Somerford Keynes: Anglo-Saxon north doorway; right (2) Coln St Aldwyns: beast's head stop to hood moulding on Norman south doorway.

3 Elkstone: Norman quadripartite vault in sanctuary, with belted boss to give 'feeling of security'.

4 Duntisbourne Rouse: originally Saxon with Norman chancel and crypt on sloping site.

5 Chedworth: Norman with Perpendicular south façade.

Leonard Stanley: top (6) Norman carved capital north of chancel: woman wiping Christ's feet; bottom (7) Norman carved capital south of chancel: the Nativity.

Southrop, Norman font: left (8) Synagogue, blinded, with broken staff; right (9) Temperancia overcomes Luxuria.

Left (10) Quenington: Norman north door, mid 12th century, with tympanum showing Harrowing of Hell; right (11) Windrush: Norman south doorway with beakhead enrichment.

Top left (12) South Cerney: early 14th-century sedilia corbel in Decorated chancel; right (13) Yanworth: probably 13th-century woman's head forms corbel to east respond of n. transept arch. Centre: left (14) Coates: dripmould stop to Perpendicular window in s. aisle; right (15) Quenington: 15th-century man's head – not in situ, but on N.W. wall. Bottom: left (16) Coates: lady's head dripmould stop to window in s. aisle; right (17) Cherington: corbel of Perpendicular roof, n. side of nave.

Top: *left* (18) *Barnsley: Norman grotesque on chancel corbel table inside organ chamber; right* (19) *Chedworth: grotesque on string-course of Perpendicular parapet on south.* Centre: *left* (20) *Chedworth: grotesque on parapet; right* (21) *Coates: anthropophagus with victim, 15th-century, on S.W. angle of tower.* Bottom, *Chedworth: left* (22) *gargoyle on parapet; right* (23) *15th-century anthropophagus.*

24 Stanton: with Perpendicular south aisle and porch, added when a possession of Winchcombe Abbey.

25 *Bibury: from the south, showing architecture of all periods.*

Top: left (26) Coberley: south doorway, unusual Perpendicular with cusped outer arch 'as at Gloucester'; right (27) Northleach porch: Perpendicular panelling partly glazed as in south porch at Gloucester, early 15th century. Bottom (28) Chipping Campden: the distinctive nave arcades with deeply concave mouldings and flat arches.

Northleach: top (29) east window clerestory with the rich curvilinear and ogee tracery of the late 15th century; bottom (30) nave arcades and clerestory with deeply concave mouldings as at Campden.

31 Fairford: west window and door; Late Perpendicular elegance.

32 Northleach: entrance to south porch; refinement and elegance.

33 Chipping Campden: tower; 'quality of displayed virtuosity'.

34 Fairford: windows and pinnacles on south aisle.

35 Chipping Campden: north aisle and clerestory windows.

Left (36) Cirencester tower and porch; right (37) Compton Abdale tower.

38 Withington from the south.

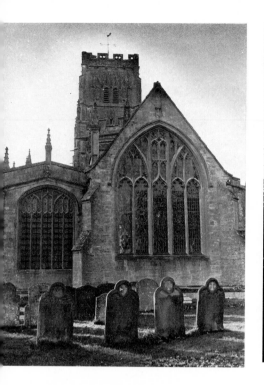

Perpendicular windows. Top: left (39) Northleach, east window: right (40) Withington, west window. Bottom: left (41) Northleach, south aisle window; right (42) Fairford, south aisle window.

COLESBOURNE

The church is in the park, on the edge of the mown lawns below the terrace of the rebuilt 'big house'. It has a curiously decaying atmosphere of past Victorian glories, in sharp contrast to the obviously vigorous new life emanating from the house on the terrace above. Colesbourne was the home of H. J. Elwes, who with Professor Henry, wrote the classic *Trees of Great Britain and Ireland*. The park and gardens still possess specimens of trees collected during Elwes' lifetime of travel. In the church are many monuments to the nineteenth-century Elwes family.

The Perpendicular west tower is built of ashlar with diagonal buttresses on the lower stage, none above, and battlements and pinnacles. The Perpendicular openings have stone quatrefoils to the belfry. The church is cruciform in plan with transepts, and a pointed chancel arch on scalloped piers, a passage squint on the north and a way to the stone pulpit on the south. The pulpit is perhaps the best thing: it is fifteenth century, vase shaped on a tall fluted octagonal stem, with one panel pierced.

The east window is by Bryans, a follower of Kempe. The other windows are by Wailes and Willement. Outside the east window is a very rare glazed tile of Edward 11's reign, depicting the crucifixion.

A ring of five bells by Abraham Rudhall 11, 1719. Complete rings by the Rudhalls are becoming increasingly rare.

RENDCOMB

This church is of extreme interest to the student and amateur of Perpendicular, as it is a complete rebuilding, all of one date and that very late as it was built in the sixteenth century. It is also well cared for, being virtually the college chapel of a boys' public school.

Sir Edmund Tame held the manor of Rendcomb. He was the son of the wool-merchant who built Fairford Church, and after he had completed his father's work *c.* 1517, he proceeded to rebuild Rendcomb.

In a way, Rendcomb follows on where Fairford stopped stylistically. The four-centred arched windows become even flatter, making it look awkward to fit in the tracery; but they are developing along their own lines and not towards the grid-pattern. The south porch is entered by what one thinks of as a Tudor doorway, in that it is rectangular with solid carved stone spandrels either side of the four-centred arch which has become stilted. There are jamb shafts like the bowtell moulding with small caps, and above is a dripmould with deep stops. The west tower has diagonal buttresses right up to the pinnacles and of course battlements; but all those grotesque medieval heads are now old-fashioned and absent. Everything is built in the best ashlar except a portion of the north wall of the nave which may be part of the original church, at any rate there are some columns buried in it.

The interior plan is a surprise and a completely new idea for the district. The nave and south aisle are almost equally broad and certainly equally long. They are divided by an arcade which has octagonal columns with concave mouldings like those at Northleach and Chipping Campden, Church Hanborough and St Helen's, Abingdon. The capitals, however, are unlike all four above examples, in that they do not have concave mouldings, and instead are more hexagonal than octagonal, with straight mouldings, forming a kind of diamond or boat shape in plan. From these spring very depressed four-centred arches with pronounced stilting. The arcade continues to the east wall dividing chancel from south chapel. There is no chancel arch or other structural division except the wooden screens.

The screens are almost identical to those at Fairford, and are probably carved by the same hand. They are a most welcome survival in a diocese rather short of woodwork. The south door also is contemporary, with original ironwork including a lockplate with arabic numerals, 1517. The timber roofs survive too, except in the chancel which was restored in 1895. There are good corbels, some with angels playing musical instruments.

The glass, or what remains of it, follows on from Fairford and has Renaissance motifs now replacing the Gothic. There are winged sibyls in the windows on the north as well as in the east window, which is mostly a restoration by George Rogers of Worcester.

We cannot leave Rendcomb without reference to the Font. It is Norman and belongs to the Hereford 'school'. It is out of place in this Perpendicular church, and, in fact, it is said not really to belong here, but to have been brought by the Guise family of Elmore. Anyway it is an interesting work of art, with an arcade containing the figures of the apostles.

A ring of six bells; three from the London foundry, fifteenth century, two dedicated to St Katherine, one to the Archangel Gabriel; the other three bells were cast at Gloucester by Thomas Mears, 1841.

NORTH CERNEY

The church and the former rectory form a beautiful group on the edge of park-like land belonging to North Cerney House. On the other side of a main road is the village.

This is probably the third church that has stood on the site. Of the first church, there are hardly any traces. It was Saxon, and the parishioners discovered the foundations when they dug a channel for the heating, and they found it was a much smaller church. Nine or ten years ago, they found further evidence of the Saxon church: they had to make a dry area round the south wall and that necessitated digging right down to the foundations and exposing them. While they were digging they found a piece of a carved crucifix, certainly pre-Norman, and probably a piece of the reredos in the Saxon church. The little piece of carving is fixed in the splay of one of the windows in the south wall of the chancel. It is very like the sculpture in Daglingworth, early eleventh century.

The second church dates from the beginning of the twelfth century. This Norman church consisted of the nave, half the present chancel and the lower part of the tower. About 1200 the chancel was extended to make it the size it is now, and they put in a new stone altar which was in scale with the new chancel; that stone altar is the one actually there now. In the sixteenth century, when the order was given that all stone altars had to go, most of them were broken up and thrown out, though sometimes they were used for other purposes, like the paving in the west door at Fairford. The North Cerney stone altar was very carefully concealed under the floor in the Lady Chapel. It is an enormous piece of work; the *mensa*, the table part, weighs one and a quarter tons, and the supporting stones of the altar were neatly arranged around it. The *mensa* was inverted so that no one would walk on the consecrated surface. No doubt the people who buried it hoped it would one day come to light again, or they hoped it would be restored in their time, but that was not to be. The people who hid it died, and it was forgotten that it was there, and it only came to light again in 1912. Some alterations were being made to the Lady Chapel, and it was decided to renew some of the worn paving stones. They were taken up and it was discovered, so in this church we have a complete medieval altar, which is very unusual in a parish church. During the next two centuries not much was done. There was some work on the tower, and the arch of the tower vestry but the church was not altered very much.

The great turning point in the story of this church is in the middle of the fifteenth century, as it is in most Cotswold churches. However, in this case, somewhere between 1450 and 1460 there was a disastrous fire which did a great deal of damage. It burnt out the Norman roof, which was a very high, steep-pitched one. We can trace the outline of the roof on the east face of the tower if we look outside. The upper regions of the tower were very badly burned; the tower acted as a chimney and the flames burnt the upper portions, and the north wall of the nave was badly damaged.

The Perpendicular roof has very finely carved corbels; the heads on the north side are said to be the reigning monarch Henry vi, which is remarkably like him, the rector of the time, who was responsible for the restoration after the fire, and the head with the coronet and handsome moustaches is believed to be the Duke of Buckingham who was the landowner, the lord of the manor. The rector, William Whitchurch, the central figure, certainly left his mark in North Cerney. It was a fortunate time for the fire to happen because there was such a tremendous lot of building going on in the second part of the fifteenth century, and not only that, there was great wealth as well which came from wool, so William Whitchurch, when he came to do the work, found the wherewithal to do it. He had the north wall rebuilt with two large windows. One of them still survives at the west end. When William Whitchurch died, glass was put in the other window to commemorate him, and later, when the transept was made, the window was taken out and put in the north wall of the transept. It has a Latin inscription at the bottom: *Pray for the soul of William Whitchurch*.

After he restored the church he began to enlarge it and he pierced the south wall, which was the Norman wall, and built the Lady Chapel. Then he died, and was followed by another priest who threw out the north transept, and had this lovely chapel made, dedicated to St Catherine, patron saint of the wool-merchants. In many Cotswold churches there are Catherine altars and Catherine chapels. By the end of the fifteenth century the work was almost finished, and the shape of the church – cruciform – was as we see it today. The Lady Chapel has a good east window, c. 1470. It has glass with the sun badge of York, the six radiant suns at the top and the two large ones down below. When we get the sun badge in glass, we can date it; it means that it was made between 1461 and 1485, when the House of York was in power. In 1485 was the Battle of Bosworth; the two Houses were joined and the Tudor period begins. The colours are fine: the blue in the central figure is attractive and do notice the little jewels in the hem of Our Lady's dress. The three carved figures are more or less the same date as the glass – late fifteenth century. They, of course, came from the Continent because any images that might have been in the church would have been lost in the sixteenth century. They look as if they have been made for this altar, in scale and so attractive. St Martin is cutting his cloak – the legend is that he gave half his cloak to a beggar. The other is St Urban holding a bunch of grapes; but there is a curious mistake because the man who carved it confused him with Urban the Great and gave him a tiara.

The High Altar is normally covered with a frontal, which is made of fine material woven for Chartres Cathedral before 1914. It is beautiful work, very heavy and rich. The reredos was designed by F. C. Eden, with Our Lord seated in Majesty and the saints coming in on either side to receive their crowns and a quotation at the bottom from one of the All Saints' lessons: 'They shall receive a glorious kingdom and crowns of gold from the hands of their Lord.'

We may notice in this church what a number of candelabra there are. The side ones are Flemish brass of the seventeenth century, and until 17 or 18 years ago the church was lit entirely by candle. Electric lighting had been kept out of the church even though it had been in the village some time; but there came a time when the candle bill got so expensive that electric lighting had to come. It was planned by Stephen Dykes Bower, who would not allow any of these 'motor headlamps' we sometimes see in churches, and we notice in the nave that there are very pleasant brackets which give just a soft light.

The Queen Anne arms were stolen and the arms we see now are the arms of our present Queen made from the proceeds of the insurance money.

The processional cross is early fourteenth century. It came to this church from France; but it is Italian work. The pulpit is *c.* 1480. The bowl is carved out of one piece of stone, deeply undercut. The lily pattern resembles carving above the altar at Magdalen College, Oxford, carried out by Burford masons. The lectern is also about the same date; but like so many other things in this church, came from the Continent. The top part of the lectern is Flemish brass and it stands on a Spanish steel pedestal; the belief is that when the Low Countries were dominated by Spain, a Spanish notable or officer took a fancy to this very fine brass work, a spirited-looking eagle, took it to Spain and had this base made for it. The extraordinary thing is how it was found in a junk yard in Gloucester but no one knows how it got there.

The east window in the Catherine Chapel commemorates a parish priest who was here after William Whitchurch died. He was not the rector, but a curate here, and again there is a Latin inscription: *Pray for the soul of John Bicot*. The colours have faded in this window because at one time when it was releaded the glass was replaced the wrong way and it weathered badly; but it is the right way round now. The altar frontal and reredos were designed by F. C. Eden, but the altar itself is seventeenth century and was formerly the main altar of the church. The piece of furniture we see here is a vestment press made of cypress wood and also designed for the church by Eden.

The organ started life as a barrel organ in the west gallery. You turned a handle and it played a couple of dozen tunes. It was an old Walker barrel organ, made in the eighteenth century, but around 1870 it was beginning to fail and did not always produce the right tunes. A new organ chamber was built with a vestry underneath, and the heating apparatus below that. The organ was converted to a hand-blown manual organ, and it stayed like that without alteration until the electric lighting was put in the church. The electric blower was attached, and the organ was enlarged by the addition of a couple of stops, and decorated by Dykes Bower and William Butchart from Westminster Abbey.

The rood loft is comparatively modern. It was designed by Eden, who had a wood-craftsman trained to do the work. The craftsman died soon after; but he was a clever man and carved it in North Cerney with oak from Rendcomb. The two side figures were made at the time, but the centre figure of Christ on the Cross dates from about 1600. It is Italian and came to this church almost by accident. Every year Mr W. I. Croome, who was church warden and who was behind many of the changes that took place in the church, the architect who planned this work, and the parish priest Mr De la Hey, used to go to the Continent, searching around for treasures. On one occasion they were in an antique shop in the north of Italy. Mr De la Hey, who was very short-sighted, was groping his way round the shop when he stumbled and fell over a packing case. The other two, thinking he had hurt himself, and rushing to help him to his feet, noticed that he had dislodged the cover of the packing case; inside they saw this figure of Christ. The screen, designed by Eden, leading into the Lady Chapel, was carved *c*. 1914 by Lawrence Turner.

The east window is not very good; but the windows designed by Eden, the south one with St Nicholas, and in the sacristy, and the big window in the Lady Chapel, with all the arms of those who lived in North Cerney House, including the Croome arms, are attractive.

Many visitors come to see the incised drawings on the wall. One is a manticore, a fabulous beast with the hindquarters and tail of a lion and the head and arms of a man. We are pretty certain it is post-Reformation. It does not seem to have any significance; no one knows why it was carved on the church and it is generally supposed that someone skilled in brasswork had found a book of illustrations. On one of the tower buttresses there is another incised figure of a leopard, obviously by the same hand.

The churchyard Cross is fourteenth century and dates from the time when there were no stone memorials to mark the graves, but just the Cross as a memorial for all who were buried in the church-yard. Burials in medieval times took place on the south side; there was a great fear of the north side and no burials took place there. The coffin was taken out through the north door; it still is at North Cerney and that is the only time the door is used. Burials now take place on all sides, in any case the south side is full. In medieval times they started at one end and worked through, and then they went back to the beginning so the same ground was used over and over again. Thousands of burials must have taken place in this piece of churchyard; but when people started putting up stones in the seventeenth and eighteenth centuries, that made it difficult to re-use the ground.

A ring of six bells; four by Abraham Rudhall 1, 1714; one by John Rudhall, 1820, and the treble by Messrs. Warner, 1863.

BAGENDON

This is an attractive and interesting little church, often subjected to flooding. The lower part of the tower is Norman, and so are the tower entrance, the tiny stairway, the windows and sound holes, so small and so many in number, pierced through solid stone for the most part. There are off-sets to support two floors, and the lower chamber has a stone trough, carved out of a single block of stone, built into the wall and with an outside drain. The tower, therefore, contained two upstairs rooms or priests' chambers. The church was first held by Llanthony Priory in Gloucester. Later when the Weavers' Guild in Cirencester had it, priests would be sent to take services on Sundays and Holy Days, and they would be able to camp in the two chambers set up in the tower.

The north arcade of three bays is Late Norman and has cylindrical piers, carved capitals, round arches with two chamfered orders, and a hood-mould. Apart from the Decorated window there are no particular alterations until the period of the Weavers' Guild, when the chancel was rebuilt *c.* 1460–70, as were the south door and porch, the windows in the nave and the diagonal buttresses of the tower. In the south window of the chancel are bits of medieval glass, Tudor roses, St Catherine's Wheel and the word *Kaerina,* and a latin reference to the 'priests of the chantry of the Holy Trinity'. The Trinity Chapel in Cirencester Church was the Weavers' Chapel.

When the floor levels were altered, some tombstones were moved, and they now stand inside the tower against the walls. One praises the son who paid for it. 'A dutiful son I have left behind: no man on earth could ever be more kind.'

A static chime of five bells by Gillett and Johnston, 1897. Two medieval clappers from the former bells are displayed in the church.

BAUNTON

This little church belonged to Cirencester Abbey till the Dissolution. It has a plain Norman chancel arch but no east window. Part of the rood screen has been made into a reredos. The Perpendicular south porch has a niche on its east wall and there is Tudor iron-work on the door; but the chief interest of the church is the splendidly preserved wall-painting of St Christopher on the interior wall opposite. He is depicted wading through a stream with green and brown fishes, and he has a red cloak with dark green and grey tunic. There is a landscape of trees and churches and a windmill. The next most interesting possession is a fifteenth-century embroidered altar frontal with the rebus of the priest's and place names, and subjects appliquéd, upon alternate panels of brown and yellow damask.

In the open western turret hang two bells by Thomas Rudhall, 1776.

STRATTON

Even nearer to Cirencester is the small, originally Norman church of St Peter at Stratton now altered and scraped disastrously. There is, however, a Tree of Life tympanum and a dog-tooth lintel over the south door. The pulpit is a successful introduction from elsewhere.

CIRENCESTER

The abbey was built partly on the site of the Saxon church, but the parish church, by far the largest and most splendid church in the Cotswolds, was placed just to the south of it, both being foundations of Henry I, *c*. 1120. Nothing remains of the abbey, and very little of the Norman church except the blocked openings in the east wall of what was then the south transept and is now the wall dividing the south aisle and the chapel or vestry behind the organ. One of these openings was fractionally opened to receive the Anne Boleyn cup, and the one high up is partly obscured by a Royal Arms. The proof of the existence of transepts in the Norman church is also to be found on the north side where there are two Early English entrance arches from the west to the Lady and Catherine Chapels, which could only have opened from a pre-existing transept. There must, therefore, have been a great deal of twelfth-century building in Cirencester as there were large churches both in the abbey and in the town, and it is regrettable we know next to nothing about them. By 1191, the abbot possessed the manor, and the castle had been sacked, never to be rebuilt. Monastic influence henceforth was always so strong the townspeople had difficulty in maintaining any separate identity.

Alterations carried out in the thirteenth century were mostly superseded during the following 200 years of the Perpendicular period. The east windows of the chancel and south chapel, however, date from *c*. 1300, and the chancel arch from about 50 years later.

The first major Perpendicular work was the tower, which was begun *c*. 1400 and was therefore fairly early as Cotswold Perpendicular towers go. It looks rather massive, partly because the middle stage is elaborately panelled with a heavy rectangular moulded 'frame' and buttresses at right-angles. The upper stage is also panelled and has arched opening with strongly vertical mullions and diagonal buttresses, crowned by an embattled parapet and large pinnacles, all of which seem very much more slender and insubstantial when we climb up it. A spire was evidently intended; but instead the builders felt they were forced to put large buttresses up against it on the south-west. However, the foundations seem quite secure, and go through the Roman road on which it is built. The money for it came from Henry IV, so the tale is told, as he was pleased with Cirencester folk for quelling the Rebellion of the Earls.

Circa 1430–60 saw the building of the elaborate chapel on the north in honour of the Trinity and for the use of the Guild of Weavers, by two Yorkist squires, Dixton and Prelatte. The arcade from the north aisle has piers of four shafts and four hollows, and the Yorkist badges of Falcon and Fetterlock can be seen on the apex of each arch on the inside. The chapel has a good contemporary roof, and has recently been restored in memory of William Parry Cripps. Arrangements have been made so that the brasses of Dixton, Prelatte and the rest can be rubbed from replicas at the opposite end of the chapel to where the originals rest behind the altar, which now has rails by Randoll Blacking moved from a redundant church. The contemporary Garstang chapel is contained in the south aisle, but even so the church had now become quite enormous. In *c.* 1450 the Lady Chapel was rebuilt in Perpendicular and soon afterwards the Chapel of St Catherine was enlarged; its stone fan vault is dated 1508. The great south porch is *c.* 1490, though it was partly rebuilt in 1831–33. The final and most significant change is the rebuilding of the nave, 1516–30, which became the tallest of any Cotswold church, perhaps of any Perpendicular church anywhere. The arcade piers are compound, with thin shafts and consequently tiny capitals, but these have hollow facets and so achieve the same kind of appearance as those elsewhere in the Cotswolds, like Northleach and Campden. Continuous pilasters also run up between the clerestory windows; thin though they are, they have the same effect as those at Northleach and Campden. Finally, there are the similar great clerestory windows, so full of light, including a very large one over the chancel arch, which has Henry VIII's arms carved over it. The exterior was finished with the most delicate pierced battlements which are far more elaborate than elsewhere in the Cotswolds and resemble St George's Chapel, Windsor Castle. On the string-course are the famous stone figures showing the Whitsun Ale Procession with many musical instruments; but they are difficult to see from the ground. No more will be said here about the Perpendicular architecture of this church as it has already been described in the introduction; there are however monuments and furnishings of great interest.

At the Reformation all 42 windows were filled with stained glass. In 1712 there was still fine glass in most of the windows; but by the end of the century it had become fragmentary because the lead cames had given way. All that remains is the glass in the splendid south-west window with saints and donors, and glass from Sidding-ton in the east window, besides considerable fragments in the traceries and elsewhere. Some of the nineteenth-century glass by Hardman is good, also the east window by Warrington in St Catherine's Chapel.

All the screens show the Midland characteristic of pierced carving between the transom and solid panel beneath. There is a carved and painted stone pre-Reformation pulpit.

Besides the brasses in the Trinity Chapel there are some in the Lady Chapel, where there is also the large Jacobean canopied tomb of Humfry Bridges by Baldwin of Stroud, the reclining effigy of Thomas Master, 1680, and a tablet to Samuel Rudder the county historian.

The great brass chandeliers show Dutch influence but were made in Bristol in 1701.

It is known that there were bells in Cirencester tower in 1499 for 'Agnes Benett, widowe, of Cisciter' whose will was proved on 14 February of that year makes various bequests regarding the bells. In the Vestry Book mention is made of recasting the bells in 1634 and Anthony à Wood tells of a ring of eight in 1678. It is probable that these were augmented to ten in 1713, for the present third cast by Abraham Rudhall of Gloucester bears that date, and then to 12 in 1722, the date of both trebles. At various times during the eighteenth century the famous Rudhall family recast most of the bells; in the Gloucester Records Office there exists the articles of agreement made in 1744 by James Brown of Cirencester, Innholder, and Thomas Vaisey of Cirencester, Maltster, on the one part, and Abel Rudhall of the City of Gloucester, Bellfounder, of the other part for the re-casting 'in a workmanlike manner the Tenth Bell of the ring of Bells'. Unfortunately during the last 80 years two of the bells have cracked, the ninth being recast by John Taylor & Company of Lough-borough in 1895, when the whole ring was fitted with new gear, and the oak frame in which the bells were hung by William Hinton, the then Cirencester tower captain, in 1867, was considerably streng-thened. At the same time, the thirteenth bell, a flat 6th was added, the gift of the Cirencester Society in London. In 1952 it was necessary to recast the 11th.

Some of them bear stock incriptions which appear on countless Rudhall bells, 'PROSPERITY TO THIS PLACE', 'PROSPERITY TO THE CHURCH OF ENGLAND', 'PROSPERITY TO ALL OUR BENEFACTORS', and the names of churchwardens of the time.

Cirencester Church has contained a ring of 12 bells for a longer period of time than any other church in the country and some ancient customs are still observed. The 'Pancake Bell' is sounded on Shrove Tuesday; on 29 May the bells are rung at 6.00 a.m. to mark the restoration of the Monarchy in 1660, and until recently the minor eight were rung half-muffled on Holy Innocents Day.

The organ (1790) is by Samuel Green and was re-built by 'Father' Willis, 1895–6. The case is by Gilbert Scott.

WATERMOOR

Watermoor, which is part of Cirencester, had its own church built in 1847–51 by Sir George Gilbert Scott, in random coursed Forest marble, with a tower having straight buttresses, bell openings with plate tracery and a spire. In his book on building in 1857 Scott says 'in the Cotswolds rubble stone should be used, in Bath or Paris freestone'. Forest marble comes from the Oxfordshire border and is limestone of the great oolite. Inside, the church has an immediate appeal, with a rather dark but comforting atmosphere, highlighted by triple lancets, very narrow and brilliant in the east above a coloured and gilded reredos, also by Scott.

The stone carving and ornaments are elaborate. Each pier and capital in the nave is different and, for instance, we are told that at the time of the building there lived at Watermoor House an Admiral Talbot who had a pew on the north side of the nave, and the sculptor, in carving the nearest capital, introduced a stone Noah's Ark into the foliage in allusion to the Admiral's nautical profession.[1] Watermoor House had been built in *c.* 1835 by the famous Savannah architect William Jay[2] for Joseph Randolph Mullings (MP for Cirencester 1848–59) but in 1850 it was let to the Admiral. Noah's Ark also appears in the east rose window of the north chancel aisle; the glass is mostly by Hardman, and there is at present the possibility of the introduction of yet more stained glass. There is a very woody roof with dormers to let in what light there is. The church was built in anticipation of an increase in population and building, and was the result indeed of the Oxford Movement. Had not the Cirencester curate, E. E. Estcourt, been commissioning a chalice from Hardman, and private crucifixes to be kept by ladies in locked boxes?

There is a ring of eight bells by Messrs. J. Taylor and Company, one dated 1887, five 1889 and two 1901.

References

1 W. St Clair Baddeley, *History of Cirencester*, p. 328
2 Jane Aiken Hodge, *Savannah Purchase.*

PRESTON

The Perpendicular tower is rather squat, otherwise it has most of the Cotswold characteristics: diagonal buttresses with string-courses round them, bell opening with the mullion in the middle, stair turret to the belfry stage; but there is not much of a base plinth. Far more interesting, however, is the bellcote over the nave gable, which is one of the best examples, fourteenth century with two stone tiers, little buttresses, and pinnacles, and space for three bells in ogee-headed openings.

The church is mostly Decorated; but over-restored. As we go in through the south porch, which has a distinctive trefoil arch, we may notice on our right there is a fine gravestone in the churchyard, probably fourteenth century. Inside the porch on the east wall is the niche we are accustomed to look for in churches round here. The Perpendicular west window gives light to the nave, which has a very low chancel arch of the thirteenth century. On either side are transepts with Decorated windows, originally of course, chapels, the piscinas and squints of which remain. The chancel is mostly nineteenth century, and the general appearance is colourless, though not without attraction.

In the tower is a ring of five bells; four of them by Thomas Rudhall, 1781; the other by Llewellins and James, 1908.

SIDDINGTON

This is an interesting church for several reasons; there are unique Norman remains, including the sculptured south doorway, chancel arch and font, and a Perpendicular chantry chapel which was once magnificent.

The church stands in what was formerly a farm nucleus and is now a horse-riding centre; however it is possible to drive up to the churchyard gate. Immediately on the left is a barn which dates from as early as *c.* 1200. The church was given to the Knights Hospitaller of Quenington by one Jordan de Clinton in *c.* 1200.[1] The barn has structural details attributable to the first half of the thirteenth century, and was probably built by the Knights soon after they received the property.[2]

The church has rather a nineteenth-century look from here, with its south tower and broach spire which were presumably built in 1864 by Henry Woodyer. However, immediately we enter the south porch we are faced by the carved Norman doorway, with its inner arch of beakheads, very well preserved, *c.* 1150. Here is perhaps an example of medieval humour; one creature is holding the snouts of his neighbours who are giving him curiously comical side-long glances. These beakheads are very similar to those ones in exactly the same position at Elkstone. In the tympanum Christ is handing the Key to St Peter, and Prof. Zarnecki thinks the third figure represents the donor, which would probably be unique, unless such a representation has hitherto been unrecognized.

On entering the church we are confronted by the font, also Norman and constructed like a tall cylinder, big enough for adult baptism? The chancel arch has chevron mouldings and is pointed, and so should be late Norman or transitional, with curled beast heads at the ends of the hood-mould surmounted by pellet or limpet-shell ornaments.

The north aisle was built by Edmund Langley *c.* 1470. His dates are 1450–1500. This once-beautiful chapel has been mutilated by the removal of the stained glass from the east window to the east window of Cirencester church, and the placing of the organ pipes in an insensitive manner in front of it. The first thing should be to remove the organ; getting the glass back is more controversial. There is a coloured plate from Lysons' book showing the glass as it was. Soon afterwards, *c.* 1800, the Lord Bathurst of the day caused it to be removed and the glazier, when remonstration was brought to his attention, is supposed to have said 'The Lord is on my side, I do not fear what man may do unto me'. Lysons, anyway, was on the Lord's side for he arranged the glass in the east window at Cirencester, where the church's own glass had got into a bad state. Edmund Langley's ancestors are shown kneeling and in armour, and also his first wife, the daughter of John Tame, who rebuilt Fairford church.

She, and her successor in Edmund Langley's bed, have the butterfly head-dresses fashionable in the reign of Edward iv (1471–83). In 1867 the Rev. the Hon. J. Gifford applied for the return of the glass, and the Cirencester Vestry passed a resolution that it should be returned when suitably replaced, knowing no doubt, that that would never be, and they were probably right.[3]

The arch of the East Window in the Langley chapel, which even with clear glass deserves to be seen much better, is four-centred, with three lights, the outer having cinquefoil tracery and the central light, where the Virgin and child would have been, having a slightly lower trefoiled head surmounted by a pair of lozenges. On one side are rich canopied niches for images and on the other side a piscina. On the north wall of the aisle are three tomb recesses with matrices for brasses of the Langley family, alas robbed, and above there are two five-light windows and towards the east a seven-light window, all with straight heads, and cinquefoil headed lights. The chapel has an embattled parapet, and according to an early nineteenth-century drawing the tower was then at the west end of the aisle. The Perpendicular roof has angel supporters, and we still get some idea of the original beauty of this rich man's gift to the church 'in honour of the Salutation of the Virgin'.

A ring of six bells by Messrs. Warner, 1879.

References

1 L. Larking, *The Knights Hospitaller of England*, Camden Society, 1857. p. 28.
2 Cecil A. Hewett *Country Life* article, 30. Dec. 1971
3 Part of the glass was returned to Siddington; but it was never used, and after about 40 years it was successfully reclaimed by Cirencester. A letter to this effect by Archdeacon Sinclair is preserved in the Bingham Library.

SOUTH CERNEY

The understanding of the sequence of building in this church is complicated by the alterations carried out in 1862 by the architect J. P. St Aubyn, who added the south aisle and extended the nave one bay to the west, thus causing the west window, a splendid piece of reticulated tracery, and the south doorway to be taken down and rebuilt.

The south doorway is another example of the local Norman school of sculpture, and resembles the south doorway at Quenington. The arch of three orders has a roll-moulding with beakheads, a simplified form of which is carried down the jamb shafts, a chevron order at right angles to the wall and a hood-mould decorated with flower heads and big beast head stops. The inner order, abaci, and capitals are carved in low relief and considerably weathered. The chief resemblance to Quenington lies in the clasping beakheads continuing down the jamb shafts; but there is no tympanum *in situ,* and the Quenington tympanum is, of course, all of one piece with the composition. The carving above the door resembles the north door at Quenington, the subject of the tympanum of which is the Harrowing of Hell. There is also another carving of Christ in Majesty, a more usual subject for twelfth-century tympana. The late Professor David Talbot Rice wrote that the Quenington sculptures were assigned with a high degree of probability to the reign of Stephen, 1134–54, and that the South Cerney work may be assigned to the same school 'though it is probably rather earlier in date'.[1]

The Norman plan of the church is retained with its central tower, and other Norman details. The pointed Transitional tower arches of the crossing have keel-moulding on the piers and the capitals show trumpet scallops and crockets. The tower originally had a spire, but this St Aubyn did not rebuild. In the chancel the east window is Decorated with ballflower (early fourteenth century) and the priest's doors north and south have ogee arches with ballflower. It is altogether a beautiful chancel; the double piscina has the most lovely carving with a vaulted canopy. The church belonged to St Peter's Abbey, Gloucester, which we suppose may account for this Decorated work, when we think of the ballflower in the south aisle windows at Gloucester.

Preserved in a case in the north wall are two fragments of a crucifixion discovered in September 1913 walled up in the church. Geoffrey Grigson thinks the head of Christ 'is one of the best things in any English church'. The original wood was covered with gesso, the surface painted in natural colours. The nearest example of comparable sculpture is to be found at Leonard Stanley, where there is a capital carved with Christ (having his feet wiped by Mary Magdalen) whose head resembles this one in style. It is suggested it might be a mid-twelfth century Spanish work brought home by a pilgrim to the shrine of Santiago de Compostela. The way the beard curls in particular is similar to other Spanish examples. The Leonard Stanley capital is nearer to the Herefordshire school of sculpture than anything else in the Cotswolds, and that school, active between 1140–60, was directly influenced by the local knight who visited Compostela, and came back full of ideas which were put into practice.

There do not seem to have been great alterations in Perpendicular times; but the east end of the nineteenth-century south aisle evidently existed as a chantry chapel.

In the usually well-kept churchyard a stone to William Hinton reads

> *As I was riding in the night*
> *On a common, for want of light*
> *Off my horse I was tossed*
> *Into the mill tail, my life I lost*

A ring of six bells, three of which date from the present century; the others are by Abraham Rudhall 11, 1721. In addition is a saunce by Edward Neal, 1676.

Reference

1 D. Talbot Rice English Art 871–1100 1952 quoting Soc. Ant. Journ. XV (1935), 203.

TRIBUTARY OF THE CHURN
The Dunt
Duntisbourne Abbots, Duntisbourne Rouse, Daglingworth

The Duntisbournes. The villages of Duntisbourne Abbots and Duntisbourne Rouse lie in the delightful valley of the River Dunt, which runs to the west of and parallel to Ermin Street, between Cirencester and Birdlip. Dunt himself was a Saxon Chief who lived at Brimpsfield. The second names of the villages were added after the Conquest to differentiate between lands in Duntisbourne owned by the Abbot of Gloucester, and by a Breton Knight named le Rous. The third village, which has no church, Duntisbourne Leer, belonged to the monks of Lyre in Normandy.

DUNTISBOURNE ROUSE

The church is situated on a rather steep bank so that it has been possible to construct a crypt under the chancel. At the west is the small saddleback roofed tower which is what we see first as we approach from the road and are immediately struck by the extremely small scale of the building.

No original windows have survived to help in the dating of the nave, but the long-and-short west quoins are of very large stones and the blocked north door has massive jamb stones. The triangular-headed south doorway still has a certain rude simplicity, and it is these features rather than the herring-bone masonry, which all now think was used both sides of the Conquest, that suggest the nave has a Saxon origin. The chancel is Norman, and the crypt below has a tunnel vault and a simple early-Norman east window. The south-west window of the nave is a pretty two-light Perpendicular insertion. The upper stage of the tower is dated 1587.

As we go inside we are struck by its dignity. The walls are lime-washed, clean and light. The floor is of stone. The roof has braced collars and moulded tiebeams and is strengthened with wind-braces. There are panelled box pews, Victorian bracket lights with brass ornaments, and one large eighteenth-century tablet by the local mason Richard Mills. (Nathaniel Haines, died 1784.)

The chancel bears evidence of a complete scheme of painting of *c.* 1200, plus or minus ten years (or perhaps it would be safer to say early thirteenth century). What survives is purely decorative and is now confined to the north wall, though there are traces of it round the twelfth-century window on the south and the return walls of the chancel arch, east face. The decoration consists of a double-line masonry pattern, both vertical and horizontal joints, with two pierced six-petalled flowers on long vertical stalks curved over at the top rising from the centre of each block. This is in dark red ochre, so dark as to be almost a purple and arguing a high iron content in the impregnated clay from which it was obtained, and heating of the material to a high temperature to obtain the dark colour. This terminates at about 5 ft. from the ground in a very simple scroll band between two bordering lines in a light red. Below this is round-headed arcading, the arches alternately red and white, and supported on plain, slender columns with simple, scalloped capitals. In each spandrel of the arcading there was a human head or grotesque. These figures face each other across the arches, but are fragmentary.

The original twelfth-century window has a continuation of the scroll and masonry pattern on the splays. The arch of the window reveal is supported by painted capitals and the stones of the arch itself are picked out in alternate red and white blocks.

The east wall of the chancel has been entirely replastered and a modern 'Norman' window inserted in the centre.

There is no painting on the barrel vault or side walls of the crypt. The only entry now is by a modern doorway, down steps from the churchyard, but originally it was by internal stairs coming up into the nave, below and slightly in front of the present pulpit.

The original deeply splayed unglazed east window remains un-altered. In two places slight traces of a double-line masonry pattern were found by Clive Rouse and the careful removal of lime-wash in the areas of wall flanking the east window disclosed fragmentary remains of two figures, which must have corresponded to those formerly on the east wall of the chancel above.

The Cotswolds are generally rather short of church wood-work, but in the chancel there are stalls with carved misericords, of grotesque heads and vine leaves. Such things are usually associated with collegiate churches and would seem unnecessary here, so per-haps they came from Cirencester Abbey after the Dissolution.[1]

The church was not restored till the 1930s, when the work was carried out by Sidney Gambier-Parry who possessed (as we would expect from the architect member of that family) great taste and much knowledge.

In the churchyard there is a table tomb on which is a very early brass plate with an inscription worth reading.

'An Elegie of Elizabeth Jefferies widow of John Jefferies of Dunsborne upon his death, who deceased the XII day of September 1611.'

In the days of absentee rectors in the eighteenth and early nine-teenth centuries, the new rectory was occupied by curates. Joseph Sisson was there from 1834 to 1840, when he moved to Barnsley. Sisson was certainly resident, as we learn from a delightful auto-biography by the taxidermist Henry White called *A Record of My Life*, which describes how the Bagendon farm-labourer's son came to Duntisbourne Abbots to school, and then got a job with the Rev. Dr Sisson, Curate of Duntisbourne Rouse. His duties were to drive a donkey cart to Cirencester twice a week, wait at table, clean knives and boots, and care for the garden and three pigs, for doing which he received £2 for the first year. A charming illustration called 'First

Appearance in Livery before his employers' shows him in 'white stockings, black plush breeches buckled at the knee, brimstone-coloured waistcoat and blue pigeon-tailed coat.' One of his duties was to follow the family to church, carrying his master's surplice. The appearance of this youth in his splendid new clothes 'caused uproar' among the village children, who had never seen anything like it.

Two bells; one mid-fourteenth century, the other early fifteenth century; both from the Bristol foundry.

References

1 Anne Carver, *The Story of Duntisbourne Rouse*

DUNTISBOURNE ABBOTS

The church is on a bank in the centre of the village. A path lined on either side with eighteenth-century headstones leads from the swinging lych-gate to the south porch. Beyond we can see that a lot of the tombstones are flat monoliths, one on top of another, which seems a local idiosyncrasy, and the churchyard is very tidy. The exterior of the church is simple with a small saddleback western tower, Norman at the bottom, later higher up. The church was unfortunately restored by Waller, that arch-scraper, in 1872, and so the inside is an aesthetic mess, with the most dreary of dark Victorian stained glass windows whose only merit is that they will open (in the summer) to let in some light. The chancel arch is a triplet of 1872, quite unsuitable for a Cotswold church, though possibly good for worship. The Arts and Crafts brass 1914 War Memorial has good lettering and local wild flowers. Do look at the south door with its medieval ironwork and handsome fifteenth-century closing ring as you go out, and of course admire the font which is Norman ornamented in low relief with trelobed foliage.

Three bells; one by Edward Neale, 1658; the others by Abel Rudhall, 1737 and 1751. Bellframe largely medieval.

DAGLINGWORTH

This small Cotswold church contains Anglo-Saxon sculptures which to some people are among the most moving archaic sculptures in England. The fabric of the church was over-restored in the nineteenth century, and only the south wall of the Saxon nave survives, together with long-and-short work at all its angles, except the north-west. Over the doorway is a very fine Saxon sundial, and the door itself is a good example of fifteenth-century woodwork.

As we approach from the west, the Perpendicular tower looks a bit stumpy, though it makes a splendid group with the Georgian house next door. It has diagonal buttresses, battlements and Perpendicular openings and mouldings. Inside the church the walls are lime-washed and the floor stone-flagged. There is plenty of light and the Victorian stained glass figures of the Crucifixion now float in clear glass in the east window. The round piers of the north arcade have scalloped overhanging capitals, and although rebuilt, are typical of so many Norman arcades in the Cotswolds.

We can now look at the Saxon sculpture. This is one of the shrines of art in England. Over the pulpit is a quite small Crucifixion, which was formerly attached to the exterior of the east wall of the chancel, and there are three more pieces, *c.* 1050, all carved by a local Saxon, in the Byzantine tradition, but in one case with a Syrian origin, for Christ is not flanked by the Virgin and St John as is usual in Byzantine art, but by the soldiers Longinus and Stephaton, one bearing the spear and the scourge, and the other the sponge of vinegar. The other two are St Peter with his key, and Christ seated in judgement; both are wearing a long robe with a knotted girdle and are perhaps the most moving in their simple dignity.

The 'English altar' and reredos are by Randoll Blacking, 1951; made of sumptuous fabrics.

The best of the tablets, and a very Baroque one, was put up by Mary Webb in 1731, just next the pulpit.

The churchyard has chest tombs and headstones, and is entered between stone gateposts with ball finials.

Of the ring of four bells two are by Abraham Rudhall II, 1720; the others were recast in the nineteenth century.

COTHELN VALLEY

Withington, Yanworth, Stowell, Chedworth, Coln St Dennis, Coln Rogers, Winson, Bibury, Coln St Aldwyns, Hatherop, Quenington, Fairford

This valley is perhaps the best known, with the most typically Cotswold atmosphere, private and remote in parts, and yet containing the much-visited but still beautiful and unspoiled village of Bibury.

WITHINGTON

The church is a typical example of an important Cotswold church in that it can be inferred that it existed in Saxon times (a resident priest being mentioned in the Domesday Book), it was completely rebuilt in the twelfth century on the usual Norman plan with nave, low central tower, and short chancel, and it was altered in the fifteenth century when the Perpendicular clerestory and higher tower were added. Other usual features for a noble church with this history are the richness of the carving on the Norman south doorway, the lengthening of the chancel in the thirteenth century, the addition of a fourteeenth-century south transept with a Decorated window, and alas, the frightful scraping it endured in the 1872 restoration. What is more unusual, however, is that the manor and patronage belonged to the Bishop of Worcester right up till the middle of the nineteenth century.

As we know that the medieval bishops of Worcester were peripatetic, the Withington manor may often have been visited. On the east side of the churchyard stands a thirteenth-century hall, incorporated into the Old Rectory, and it may therefore be surmised that this was the residence of the bishops rather than, or as well as, one of the later houses in the village. It is known for instance, that the Bishop was here for the Feast of Pentecost in 1284, and an ordination in 1286, and in 1290 it was made a prebend to his collegiate church at Westbury-on-Trym just as had been done at Blockley. There seem to have been several priests, and this was the time when the chancel was lengthened.

The Norman south doorway would appear not to be earlier than *c.* 1150. It has the same exuberance as other doorways of this local school, and is very well preserved with its three or more orders of many chevrons, and the convex moulding with four petalled flowers in a lozenge (cf. fragments to be found in the old church at Churchdown). The hood-mould has sunflowers, and ends in beast-heads. The plain jamb shafts have scalloped capitals.

The best features are, however, Perpendicular. Who paid for these alterations? It may not have been a rich layman as the lord of the manor was a bishop; but in any case the money probably came from wool. And what is the date? The tracery of the big east and west windows resembles the work of Abbot Morwent's time at St Peter's Abbey, Gloucester (1421–37). The upper stage of the tower is extremely elegant with its large bell opening having four trefoil-headed compartments, the outer ones louvred, surmounted by six small traceried lights under an ogee-shaped and crocketed hood-mould. The buttresses are not diagonal as is usual in the Cotswolds, but straight and parallel. The battlements have tall panelled pinnacles with pretty finials rising from winged gargoyles at the corners.

The five clerestory windows either side have four-centred heads, with deep hollow-moulded surrounds contrasting with the triangular-shaped buttresses in between which are capped with finials which look really late Tudor. The windows have three cinquefoiled lights, and there is a similar window inserted into the south wall of the chancel. The great east window is similar to the west window with full-blown Perpendicular tracery including the horizontal transom element in the central top light. The prototype for this window is to be found in the west windows of the aisles of Gloucester Cathedral.

The south-east window of the nave is another kind of Perpendicular window, and this must have lit a nave altar or chantry chapel; medieval glass remains in the tracery, and Victorian glass below in memory of the rector for 62 years, George Gustavus Chetwynd-Talbot, fifth son of the second Earl Talbot, born in 1810 and died in 1896, through whom the church was restored in 1872–73 by David Brandon, with such depressing results. Re-plastering would improve the atmosphere no end.

An inscription on a delightful modern tablet by Lesley South: 'Remember Walter Henry Heyden, 1889–1971, clerk to eight rectors from 1918 to 1971', accounts for all the incumbents since Chetwynd-Talbot. However, the best monument is rather high up in the south-west of the nave, to the people who lived at Cassey Compton in the seventeenth century. They are seen as if sitting in their box at the theatre, until one notices they are holding skulls and other symbols of mortality like the sands of time. It is by Edward Marshall and is signed and dated 1651.

There is a fifteenth-century oak bellframe for four bells to which Rudhall added two pits when he recast the former bells and augmented their number to six in 1738–39. (For bellframe cf. Elkstone.)

YANWORTH

The small church, with a miniature embattled tower flush with the west wall, stands in a farmyard setting in Stowell Park. It is late Norman, and remarkable for its fine-jointed ashlar exterior, and pretty grouping of roofs. Perpendicular windows have been introduced to improve the interior lighting in the fifteenth century, several with that unfortunate feature of a central mullion bisecting the window and continuing up into the apex of the arch. The churchyard is beautifully kept up. Inside, the Bishop's Chair, designed by Anthony Sanford, reflects the Laudian Communion rails.

The manor and church of Yanworth originally belonged to the Abbey of Gloucester; but in 1250 it was transferred to Winchcombe together with Hazleton, possibly owing to the influence of John de Yanworth, at that time Abbot of Winchcombe.[1]

References

1 Ulric Daubeny, *Ancient Cotswold Churches*. (1921)

STOWELL

The church here is one of a complex of well-cared-for buildings immediately at the back of Lord Vestey's mansion, but it is of very great interest, as it contains quite well-preserved fragments of twelfth-century wall-paintings.

The church is cruciform with a central tower which hardly now exists, and north and south transepts. On the north wall of the nave is a painting of *c.* 1150–1200, showing the apostles sitting in pairs within an arcade, their heads shorn like Norman monks. In the centre is the Virgin holding up her hands in astonishment at the scene below, which is of course, the Last Judgement. The apostles' feet and hands are equally expressive; but there is no Majesty left above. In the south transept there are some more fragmentary paintings, enough to show how fascinating it must have been for contemporary worshippers. Architectural details are Norman. The floors are stone-paved, and the pews all newly made by the estate carpenter.

CHEDWORTH

The twelfth-century Norman church preserves its original plan of nave with west tower and north aisle, and chancel, though there must have been an earlier church as it was given to the abbey of Lyre in Normandy soon after the Conquest by William Fitz Osborn.

By far the most striking thing about the church is, however, its Perpendicular south wall, rebuilt in the second half of the fifteenth century. In this case there is an inscription written in Latin commemorating Richard Sly (there are still people of this name in the

Cotswolds), who presumably was the benefactor for this splendid rebuilding, and the date was 1461. Sly was most likely a wealthy wool merchant, like the other benefactors in the Cotswolds at this date, though it has been suggested he was the bailiff of the Nevilles who owned the manor. On the lower face of the turret is another date, 1485, in Arabic numerals, and as at Northleach it is an early example of this usage. It was the year of the battle of Bosworth where Anne Neville's husband, Richard iii, was killed.

On the jamb of the south doorway is the date 1491. The doorway is a most notable piece of rich Perpendicular work, arranged in two planes, the outer four-centred arch standing clear of the recessed background, both with enriched spandrels, the outer open, the inner solid.

The splendid south range of five Perpendicular windows have four-centred heads in a hollow moulding, and are of three lights with cinquefoil heads, with tracery at the head and below the transoms. Two windows, however, do not go below transom level because of the necessity of accommodating the earlier porch. Above is an embattled parapet with gargoyles, and at the eastern end a pinnacle, and also the turret for the original rood loft stair.

Inside there is a stone Perpendicular pulpit like others in the Cotswolds at Northleach, North Cerney, Cirencester and Naunton, goblet shaped, and carved with traceried panels, crocketed gables, and buttresses.

The interior is very charming because these great Perpendicular windows are like a wall of clear tinted glass which reflects the light on to the plastered walls. The glass in the east window is by Curtis, Ward & Hughes in 1898, and looks like a Kempe window with angels' peacock feathered wings.

The church is approached by an ancient medieval street known as Queen Street, because here Elizabeth of York came on her way to see the Perpendicular additions. Near the gate are the graves of the Turk family, seventeenth to nineteenth century, including Methusalem Turk, 1799. The village lies not in the main valley of the Coln, but in a small one that is adjacent. Indefatigable bell-ringers fill the 'distant wolds with basic music'[1] from a ring of six bells cast by Abel Rudhall, one dated 1747, three 1738 and two 1739.

References

1 John Green in *The Cotswolds. A new study*, edited by C and A-M Hadfield.

COLN ST DENNIS

The Norman plan of the church is undisturbed, with chancel, nave and central tower. The length has not been altered as can be seen from the flat Norman buttresses at the east end of the chancel and the string-course at the west end of the nave. Norman north and south doorways survive. There must have been a stone vault in the chancel as shafts remain in the corners.

The Perpendicular replacements are the windows on the east and north of the chancel and they are the grid type common elsewhere but not what we have learned to expect in the Cotswolds, and the glass by Ward & Hughes is very poor. There is also a Perpendicular window on the south of the nave, a Perpendicular parapet, and restored Perpendicular roof which is supported on re-used Norman corbel stones, including a beakhead. People in the late medieval period with their love of grotesque heads usually respected Norman carvings.

A complete ring of five bells by Abraham Rudhall II, 1734. (cf. Colesbourne.)

COLN ROGERS

This little church is unique in the Cotswolds in that it has a Saxon nave and chancel which have survived almost intact, except for the enlargement of all but one of the original windows, the rebuilding of the east end of the chancel, and the erection of a west tower within the nave.

The distinctly Saxon features are the simple plinth, the long-and-short quoins at all the angles of the nave except the north-east, the four pilaster strips of which two have stepped bases, and the tiny, round-headed north window of the chancel with its outer face cut in a single oblong stone and outlined by a double rebate. The round-headed chancel arch and its jambs are of two plain square orders, the imposts chamfered below and enriched on their vertical faces by a simple pattern of pellets in a V-shaped groove. In the north wall of the nave a blocked doorway has an early thirteenth-century outer face with late Norman capitals and a five-foiled arch; but the doorway appears to be Saxon in origin.

The Perpendicular window in the south side of the nave has crowning tracery similar to that in the chancel east window at Northleach from whence the idea must have come. The tower is even later. The interior of the church never seems very attractive, perhaps because it is over-restored.

In the churchyard is a beautiful modern gravestone to Professor David Talbot Rice by Simon Verity in spangled Purbeck stone.

One of the three bells is by an unidentified founder whose initials were 'I.R.'; another was cast at the Gloucester foundry by someone using Rudhall's plant in 1846; the third is by Abraham Rudhall 1, 1716.

WINSON

The small ancient church stands adjacent to the Georgian manor house, the side view of which is seen from the slightly raised churchyard. We enter through an *art nouveau* iron gate. There is a nice group of identical table tombs, and a new flat slate, beautifully lettered by Bryant Fedden, commemorating Walter Field 'for fifty years carpenter and wheelwright in this parish and devoted servant of the church, died 1961'.

The south porch has a niche in its east wall, and a plain Norman doorway into the nave. There are no aisles and the chancel arch is similar to the doorways. The small chancel has Victorian decorative wall paintings; both font and pulpit are over-restored.

BIBURY

The evidence of the place-names suggests that West Saxon influence was restricted to the Thames Valley with some extension northwards along the affluent valleys of the southern Cotswolds. Bibury was named from Beage, the daughter of Earl Leppa, to whom the land was granted by the Bishop of Worcester in the eighth century,[1] and the word burh, a fortified place. It is possible therefore, that a Saxon church could date from that time, 721–43;[2] but without excavations little can be known about this.

On the north wall of the exterior of the chancel is a Saxon pilaster strip; the pilaster itself is carved with late-Saxon ornament consisting of interlacing circles, with pellets in the interstices. This interesting carved stone, one of a number found near the church in 1913, was placed in its present position when the others were presented to the British Museum. On the south side of the chancel exterior is another Saxon pilaster strip with a boldly stepped base. Close to the south porch is a deep-splayed circular window, probably the last trace of an Anglo-Saxon clerestory.[3] The two lancet windows west of this, set curiously high, have a Saxon string-course above. These indications that the Saxon church was high are reinforced inside where we find a tall narrow chancel archway with Saxon jambs and imposts, that on the north carved with foliage of Ringerike affinities, and that on the south with an upright palmate leaf and scrolled leaves at the side, like the Winchester school of illumination of the late tenth and early eleventh centuries.

The church must have had a tall long nave and a short chancel. The monks of Oseney added a north aisle. In doing this they opened, without entirely destroying, the north wall of the nave. On the north, above the arches, remain pilaster strips of the original external Saxon north wall, and towards the west, just under the present roof, is a small blocked window, high up and probably formed by the adaption of a window similar to the circular Saxon window on the south. The arcade is Late Norman, and is not continuous, but interrupted at irregular intervals by chunks of wall left standing. This probably indicates a pre-existent Saxon porticus. There is no other logical explanation, except that it came about because of gradual development, and this seems contradicted stylistically as there is very little chronological difference from east to west, although there are a variety of forms.[4]

The arches are unchamfered. The eastern respond has a beautiful capital of Canterbury type with acanthus leaves, a Romanesque descendant of classical Rome's most beautiful architectural form. The next capitals have the locally more usual trumpet scallops, and also enriched waterleaf. All this means *c.* 1180–90. The shafts are keeled which goes with such a date, so does the chevron at right angles to the wall. There is also a beast-head stop, a revival of an Anglo-Saxon form, the origin of which was Scandinavian. The immediate source for twelfth-century sculptors would have been places like Deerhurst.

The one free-standing pier is round, and has a round multi-scalloped capital, the earliest in style in the sequence. Towards the tower stop chamfers appear, and the triple chamfered arch from tower to aisle is fully Early English, later-looking really than the short arcade on the opposite side which was never continued westwards of the south doorway.

In the thirteenth century a new pointed chancel arch was placed on the Saxon imposts, piercing the Saxon string-course which originally served to support a rood. There are traces of the figure which stood on the left, the other mutilated stones are part of it, and the blocked windows may be Saxon and intended to light the rood, later given Perpendicular tracery. At the same time in the thirteenth century the chancel was lengthened and given its lancet windows.

There is hardly an ancient church in England where there is not some indication that the short earlier chancel was extended and embellished in the thirteenth century due to the concentration of theological interest upon the doctrine of the Holy Sacrament. It was marked by the decrees of the Lateran Council in 1215, the works, the writings, and the splendid hymns of St Thomas Aquinas, and the institution of the Feast of Corpus Christi. Rarely, however, do we find so noble and spacious a chancel as we have here, culminating in the triple lancets of the east wall. The chancel is also notable for the large number of aumbries or cupboards, and the little window on the south of the sacristy with original thirteenth-century glass, all of which indicate that the monks from Oseney had considerable treasure behind an altar which stood to the west of the east wall.

The Decorated windows in the north aisle were added in the fourteenth century. Then with the further prosperity of the wool trade, the Perpendicular nave roof and clerestory were added, not in the grandest manner as at Northleach, but with simple straight-headed two-light windows under an embattled parapet. The great west window is also a fairly simple and repetitive design. Maybe the lay farmers were not quite so well off here as at neighbouring places, because the manor still belonged to the Abbot of Oseney, who took quite a lot of money out of the estate. The abbot had a shepherd in Bibury even at the Dissolution; the crucked central bays of Arlington Row could have been his wool-store since *c.* 1390. In the church there are some sheeps' heads lying on the floor near the beautiful Transitional Norman font, and these may have been corbels. In the south porch, which is itself Transitional Norman of *c.* 1200, there is a niche cut into the east wall, a feature of fifteenth-century date often found in this position in the Cotswold group of churches. It was for an altar and could have been used for a poor man's light. The better-off left money for candles to be lit for their soul's good in the chantry chapels within. In Bibury there must have been such chapels in both aisles as piscinas survive here, and they would have been beside an altar. The piscina was a bowl with a drain, usually set

in a small niche, down which the water used for rinsing the cele-
brant's fingers could be poured. It also held a shelf of wood or stone
which served as a credence to carry the cruets. The Wilcox chapel
is referred to in late fifteenth-century wills; it must have been
in one or the other aisle, and both have a tomb recess in the
wall which may have been Wilcox's; but who he was is not now
known.

The church was restored by Sir Gilbert Scott in 1863. Water-colours
of 'before' and 'after' are preserved in Arlington Mill Museum. In
spite of these restorations it is remarkable how unspoiled English
churches generally were compared with churches on the Continent.
The chief visible difference in Bibury, apart from the chancel roof
which was made to look more medieval, was due to new furnishings. The box pews of course, went in favour of more religious
kneelers; the Laudian communion rails were replaced by something
more Gothic; but that in its turn has now been altered back to Neo-
Laudian rails. There was a new pulpit of stone and marble, and a
fine brass lectern by Skidmore. The east window already had glass
by Willement. The decalogue and some hatchments were moved; but
the nice eighteenth-century tablets in the chancel to the ladies of the
manor, which in themselves provide so much atmosphere and a
whiff of a more worldly past connected with such things as the Bibury
Race Club, remained.

In 1927 colourful stained glass was put into a chancel window on
the north, by Karl Parsons, showing Mr Cooper's coach from Bibury
Court, still remembered with nostalgia by the oldest inhabitants. The
church was also presented with two seventeenth-century Spanish
needlework pictures of baroque composition.

The churchyard is of special interest because of the remarkable
survival of so many excellently carved table tombs with bale tops,
and headstones with cherubs and symbolic figures of the seventeenth
and eighteenth centuries.

No church could have a more attractive and harmonious setting.

Successive vicars upheld their privilege of the Peculiar Jurisdiction of Bibury exempting them from the authority of the Bishop
of Gloucester. A lively correspondence took place between the Rev.
Sackville Cresswell and the Bishop, in which the Vicar won his
point, the bishop was prevented from making a formal visita-
tion in 1828, and Cresswell was nicknamed Bishop of Bibury. Sackville Cresswell was the luckiest of his family, being safely installed

as vicar. The others were ruined by a perfectly unnecessary law-suit, and his unfortunate brother, the Squire, ended his days in 1841 in a debtors' prison in Boulogne, instead of at Bibury Court, which was sold to Lord Sherborne. The Rev. Henry Snow of the Gilbert Scott restoration, who was married to the daughter of Canon Howman of Barnsley, built the Vicarage in 1843 and died there in 1873. Canon the Hon. Frederick George Dutton (afterwards Lord Sherborne) was vicar for the rest of the century and beyond, into living memory; Donald Taffinder has now been there 30 years.

There is a complete ring of bells by Abraham Rudhall 11, 1723. (cf. Colesbourne.)

References

1 A. H. Smith, *Place names of Gloucestershire*, Pt. I., p. 26. (1964)
2 ed. W. de G. Birch, *Cartularium Saxonicum*, London 1885–93. No. 166.
3 H. M. Taylor, *Anglo-Saxon Architecture*, Vol. I. p. 63. (1965)
4 *Buildings of England. Gloucestershire: The Cotswolds.* p. 108. (1970)

COLN ST ALDWYNS

Coln Church has a very splendid tower on the south side, which produces a curious plan, and the whole building with its various additions looks much larger from the outside than it does when we get inside. In fact it is altogether better aesthetically from the outside.

The tower is massive and ancient, Norman and Early English with straight clasping buttresses, and with a Perpendicular top stage built of fine ashlar and having a pierced parapet, and turrets with crocketed pinnacles at the angles bearing shields of arms including those of Gloucester Abbey to which the church was appropriated. The belfry openings have deep hollow mouldings. There is a string-course with friendly gargoyle faces; but to the east of the south porch, over a blocked Norman window, is the figure of a demon pursuing a man whose hand he holds in his jaws.

The late Norman south doorway, though restored and partly re-cut, has three orders with deeply undercut lozenge and chevron mouldings on keeled jamb shafts with Transitional capitals and a hood-mould terminating in beast-heads.

Big battlements run round the nave parapet. The west window has reticulated tracery. The chancel is Early English; but rather spoiled by blackish pointing. There is a sanctus bellcote.

Inside it is very dark with poor Victorian glass; it was over-restored in 1853. It must look very different to the way it did when John Keble's father was Vicar, in 1782–1835.

A saunce by Edward Neale, 1656, and a ring of eight, two of them by G. Mears and Company, 1865, the others by Abraham Rudhall, 1724–25.

HATHEROP

The church is approached from the village by a long path between the gardens of some houses and the park of Hatherop Castle. An easier way would be from the castle; but that is a girls' school. In 1850 Lord de Mauley had the architect Henry Clutton rebuild the mansion, and then the church. As a result the latter is now a curious building with a French-looking central tower, a high clere-storied Perpendicular nave, and a really splendid south chapel designed by Clutton's more famous partner William Burges in 1855, the exact year that the partners won the Lille Cathedral competition.

It is difficult to say what existed before, but the combination of Perpendicular and French Gothic is so peculiar we can only suppose there was at least a Perpendicular nave and north porch. The central tower with its Frenchified gabled roof has a corbel table very high up with grotesque heads, and some of these look as if they could be original Norman work. Above the clerestory there is a pierced para-pet of distinctly nineteenth-century character. The porch, if old, is much restored and has image niches both inside on the east wall and over the entrance arch. A far more intriguing entrance is to be found on the south side into the chapel which must be designed by that genius Burges. It has a pointed arch carved with an oak leaf trail, and hood-mould stops with mysterious beasts and foliage. Either side are round windows and the whole is overgrown with wistaria. How-ever, we cannot enter here and must return to the north porch. The interior is spacious, and lit with brilliantly coloured glass by O'Connor, and Lavers, Barraud & Westlake. The altar hangings are sumptuous, and the whole has a cared-for atmosphere. Again, however, the chapel, a mortuary for Barbara Lady de Mauley, really steals the picture with its splendid stone vault and rich carving, com-bined with the stark simplicity surrounding the elegant figure of Lady de Mauley lying on a tomb chest guarded by life-size winged angels.

One of the ring of six bells was recast by the Bonds of Burford,

1906; four are by Abraham Rudhall 1, 1715; the tenor is by Messrs. Mears, 1852. In addition are a saunce, dated 1621, and a bourdon bell by Messrs. Warner, 1868.

QUENINGTON

This church is unique in that it retains two elaborately enriched Romanesque doorways, both works of art of the greatest interest, and superior to the others in this specialized field. Their date is *c.* 1150, and therefore they were there before the manor was given to the Knights Hospitaller by Agnes de Lacy in *c.* 1193.

The south doorway is by the sculptor of the doorway at South Cerney, according to Professor Zarnecki, but the Quenington design is all of one piece and incorporates that most precious and rare tympanum of the Coronation of the Virgin, which is indeed thought to be the second example of the use of this subject, if the first is the capital from Reading Abbey, now in the Victoria and Albert Museum. The subject was Greek and apparently came to England from Greek monasteries in Italy. Compared with the Reading sculpture this is a primitive version by a provincial sculptor; but he must have had a model and it was possibly not Reading. Both probably had a model now unknown to us. The Feast of the Immaculate Conception of the Virgin was celebrated at Gloucester and Winchcombe Abbeys, less than 20 miles from Quenington.[1] Witnesses of the Coronation are two seraphs, a heavenly mansion and the Evangelist's symbolic beasts. The whole is enclosed in a chevron moulding which continues down the jambs of the doorway. The next order is that of beakheads. Round the roll of the arch they are mostly animals, but down the jamb shafts they become extremely stylized clasping tongues.

The north doorway is perhaps less homogenous but in its way even more overwhelming in its elaboration, with at least four orders. The inner arch has chevrons at right angles, farther out is a band of limpet shells. The abaci are carved with star, cable, knot and billet mouldings, and the capitals with jacks-in-the-green symbols of fertility. The outer jambs have large marguerite flowers. The tympanum shows the Harrowing of Hell, based on the apocryphal 'Gospel of Nicodemus' with Christ apparently prodding Satan, who lies on the ground. There are three other naked figures, perhaps the two Jews who were said to have risen from the dead with Christ, and a third who is half in the devil's mouth. Above is a Sun disk with a face in it, to show the 'Dayspring from on high' which pierced even the eternal darkness.[2] Above all is a much-weathered grotesque head, unrecognizable. The walls retain Norman masonry, pilasters and string-course; but the church is generally so altered it has little other interest, except the modern flowering of artistic needlewomen's kneelers. The churchyard, in a very pretty setting, is mostly cleared of gravestones.

References

1 *Journal of the Warburg Institute* XIII 1950 pp. 1 seq.
2 M. D. Anderson, *History and Imagery in British Churches.*

FAIRFORD

Fairford lies on the edge of the Thames gravels, although in every other way it is a Cotswold town, once made important by the wool-merchant John Tame who rebuilt the church during the last quarter of the fifteenth century. With the exception of the base of the early fifteenth-century central tower, the church was completely rebuilt, and fitted with glass specially made for it, which has miraculously survived. It is supposed that the Cromwellian squire Oldisworth removed the faces of some of the figures in order to seem to obey his instructions to destroy what was idolatrous.

The tower is not unlike the lower part of the tower at Cricklade; it is sturdier to look at, however, and has a telling parapet with huge open quatrefoils and pairs of diagonally set pinnacles at the corners. It is also covered in sculptures, mostly grotesque, some of which belonged to the earlier church. Four hatted figures with swords are set at each corner of the tower on the buttresses, beneath padlocks. On the south side low down, is the bold carving of a man's huge head, and a hand holding a scourge similar to one at Lechlade. Above is the relief of a griffin, and above on the parapet Tame has placed the Warwick arms, and the Yorkist Shut-Fetlock; on the east the Warwick badge, a bear-muzzled climbs a ragged staff and above this the arms of de Clare, and scissors, a hunters' horn and baldric, emblems of local occupation. On the north are a dragon and a wine vat; above the arms of Despenser, on the left Tame's merchant's mark, on the right two horse-shoes and pincers. On the west is the figure of Christ, thought to be an interesting example of late fifteenth-century art where the carvers deliberately set out to carve in primitive style. This 'Image of Pity' was popular at the time. Christ is nimbed and wears the Crown of Thorns; in His left hand is the Resurrection Cross, and the spear wound in His side is visible. Above are the armorial bearings of John Tame, a wyvern combating a lion, with on one side the shell of a salt-trader and on the other shears and gloves. The embattled parapets of all the component parts have string-courses enlivened also with spirited sculpture often copied from the old bestiaries. One particularly charming human jester dangles a leg. At regular intervals pinnacles rise from the string courses through the battlements. In December 1971 on a Sunday during Matins a sudden hurricane (like the one which blew in the west window in the reign of Queen Anne) tore along the roof tops knocking down the pinnacles and doing much damage, all of which has been most brilliantly repaired by Peter Juggins, a mason whose instincts and technique are a match for the original sculptors. The newly carved stone pinnacles look beautiful in their freshness, and Mr Juggins's ram, lamb and wyvern seem perfectly authentic, as does his Virgin and Child on the south porch.

King Henry vii had acquired in 1487 from the Countess of Warwick, daughter of the Kingmaker, 114 manors sequestrated after the battle of Barnet, and Fairford was one of 14 in the county of Gloucester. Henry's portrait is thought to appear on corbels in the contemporary churches of Chedworth and Northleach. Here his influence can be seen in the greatest treasure of all, the glass, for it is by the school of his Master Glass Painter, the Fleming, Barnard Flower.[1] A detailed account of the glass can be obtained in *The Buildings of England*, or in the church itself. John Tame intended his windows to read as a picture story from the Bible in days when few could read the written word. The brilliant colour would be as effective as coloured television is today in making an impact on the mind. The scenes from Our Lady's and Our Lord's lives are enacted before our eyes, in front of backgrounds of Perpendicular and Flemish architecture. The story begins appropriately in the Lady Chapel, and ends with the prophets on the north side of the nave, which are the best of all. The windows generally have four-centred arches fairly flat, and conventionally disciplined Perpendicular mullions dividing the tracery over ogee-headed lights with cinquefoil heads. The mullions inside have keeled ovolo mouldings combined with a concave moulding either side, and there are big hollow mouldings, particularly outside, round the frame. Some of the mullions have round bowtell mouldings and are as elegant as those of Richard

Winchcombe. The west doorway is particularly delightful with shaped stops.

The woodwork here is also of great interest as it is almost unique in the Cotswolds, just as the glass is unique in all England. The rood screen has vanished and what remains is the enclosing screen of the choir. Between the Lady Chapel and the chancel the parclose screen is worked into a timber arch surmounting the tomb of the Founder John Tame. The inscription on the brass reads:

> 'I may not pray; now pray ye
> with Paternoster and Ave
> That my pains released may be.'

The screens can be compared with those at Rendcomb also provided by Sir Edmund Tame, the Founder's son, and both bearing the pineapple emblem of Katherine of Aragon. The stalls with their carved misericords were provided for singers, but were perhaps taken from elsewhere as they do not quite fit. In 1854 J. L. Pearson provided seating similar to the choir stalls but 'not copied'. On the walls facing east are two modern tablets, one to John Keble by John Bowler, and the other to Noëlle Countess of Rothes, heroine of the *Titanic* disaster and certainly a reader of *The Christian Year*.

The High Altar was designed by Sir Ninian Comper. The Lady Altar is by Geoffrey Webb, alabaster painted and gilt, *c.* 1913, with a dorsal of blue silk damask panelled with black and gold orphreys. It was the gift of the then Lord Beauchamp and the shields show the relationship of the Lygons with the Tame family. In the corner are the recumbent effigies of Roger Lygon and his wife who was widow of Sir Edmund Tame II, erected in 1560. The Lectern in the chapel has twelfth-century feet in the form of beast-heads. On the north wall there is a small and exquisite little brass of the Blessed Trinity. High up are two crested helmets. There is fan-vaulting in the porch. In the churchyard look for the 'Egyptian' table-tomb.

A modern ring of eight bells by John Taylor and Company.

References

1 David Verey, *The Buildings of England. Gloucestershire: The Cotswolds* pp. 245–6.

THE LEACH VALLEY

Hampnett, Northleach, Aldsworth, Eastleach, Southrop,
Lechlade

This small river is immortalized by the presence of Northleach
Church, next to Cirencester the most beautiful church in the Cotswolds; 'ascetic despite its elegance, breathing an intellectual Gothic
confidence as if to dispute the need for any (foreign) Renaissance',
wrote John Green, though in what direction could Gothic architecture now develop, for it has been pushed to its absolute structural
limit, so flat are the four-centred arches they can only just hold up,
and so aerial the space contained.

HAMPNETT

A small farming community near Northleach with a very perfect
little Norman church to which has been added a splendid big Perpendicular tower at the west. The tower has diagonal buttresses to the
middle of the third stage of its ashlar walls which are crowned with
battlements and gargoyles, and pierced with four-centred arched
belfry openings. Originally, as it is a three-compartment church
like Elkstone, it probably had a small tower in the centre over the
choir. The stone quadripartite rib vault in the sanctuary survives and
the late Norman carved detail is very good including stiff stalk
capitals, and on the choir-arch capital doves drinking from a bowl
neck to neck. All this has been greatly enhanced by the Victorian
scheme of painting by Clayton & Bell and the parson Mr Wiggin.
Judging from the remains of wall painting, for instance, at Duntisbourne Rouse, it would seem that something like this would have
been done in late Norman times, and the result in any case is pleasing, and should be preserved. The sanctuary is now well lit because,
although the original small Norman east window survives, the
windows north and south have been replaced by Perpendicular
ones.

Three bells; one by John Rudhall, 1832; one by Bond, nineteenth
century; the third probably cast at the Aldbourne foundry.

The organ (1874) is by Nicholson & Co.

NORTHLEACH

John Fortey, the builder of the nave of the church and a rich wool-
merchant, died in 1458–59. Unlike Chipping Campden, the tower

was built before the nave, otherwise the two churches are so similar we are forced to think they are in the main by the same man, though Northleach nave was perhaps some decades in advance. The tower is quite early in the fifteenth century, is crowned by panelled battlements, and has four diminishing stages, and openings in the top stage in groups of four with ogee hood-moulds, and pinnacles, as at St Nicholas, Gloucester. It is not so elaborate as the later tower at Campden. Where, however, Northleach does completely take the edge off Campden is in the porch, which incidentally retains four medieval images (there is another on the east gable of the nave). The porch has a vaulted roof of two bays with plenty of tiercerons, and a polygon in the middle filled with tracery and bounded by liernes. It was built *c.* 1500 and is of two storeys (see p. 40, p. 49). The other one most like it is at Burford. The panelled walls have image brackets with corbels, one of which shows a cat fiddling to three rats. Here the windows are single lights set in most refined panels of tracery with bowtell mouldings; very pointed and yet Perpendicular. This is comparable with the earlier elegance of Richard Winchcombe.

The windows generally have chamfered mullions either hollow or ogee. The tracery of the windows is more beautiful than at Campden, particularly in the east clerestory window which has such lovely sweeping lines it is almost like an unexpected foretaste of *art nouveau*. The east window of the chancel is the more usual Perpendicular type like some at the west end of Gloucester Cathedral; in this case it has 2, 1, 2 lights. The south aisle east window has a much flatter four-centred arched head and in detail resembles the clerestory east window, and those on the south have elaborate transoms with a row of quatrefoils above four cusped ogee headed lights, features which we now recognize as being late in the development of Perpendicular tracery, and these are in fact part of the Bicknell chapel, dated 1489.

The beautiful stone was locally quarried in medieval quarries underground on the edge of the town. The interior is full of lightness and space owing to John Fortey's clerestory, and his arcades are transmogrified by their excessively concave mouldings into dynamic architecture. The original roof, *c.* 1495, has survived, unlike the one at Campden which was renewed; but much of the colour of the medieval church is missing, with the loss of the glass and wall-paintings, and even the Victorian stained glass of the east window has given place to an insipid work by Christopher Webb (1963). The liturgical arrangements are unfortunately very much in evidence with a nave altar, and seating by Sir Basil Spence replacing that of James Brooks. The chancel now called the Chapel of the Resurrection retains the triple canopied sedilia. The double Tudor rose suggests its date as being after 1486 when Henry VII married Elizabeth of York. Their Royal heads are also to be seen in the Lady Chapel corbels. Supported by a wooden table is the original *mensa*, ten feet in length. It was buried in the foot-pace at the Reformation, and now replaced *in situ*. The riddel posts and angels are by F. E. Howard and the altar frontal was designed by Sir Ninian Comper. The stone crozier heads inserted in the walling, one on each side of the chancel, are thought to refer to the fact that the church belonged to St Peter's Abbey, Gloucester up to the Dissolution. There is another *mensa* in the sacristy.

The church is well-known for the wool-merchants' brasses. There is one of a priest kneeling before the images which still survive on the porch though not in the brass, and one of Thomas Busshe, merchant of the staple of Calais; these are both sixteenth century. John Fortey's brass is an excellent example of the best period of brass engraving, and his father's which says 'Pray for ye children of Thomas Fortey', must have been the most splendid – he died in 1447, and was a 'renovator of roads and churches', the words being interspersed with stops representing a rose, a crab, sporting dogs, a snail, a pig, a hedgehog and oak leaves. Such charming details are irresistible, and add to the enchantment of one of the most dynamic examples of Perpendicular architecture in the Cotswolds, if not anywhere.

ALDSWORTH

One of the high bleak Cotswold villages in hardly a valley at all, yet not without a certain sophistication, due perhaps to the past presence of Lord Sherborne on one side and the Bibury Race Course on the other. It was also the last place to hold a flock of Cotswold sheep, Mr Garne's.

The church is remarkable. Typically, it has Norman and Perpendicular elements; but the latter are quite a *tour de force*. Approached from the north-east uphill under rather scraggy old yews which preclude the further view evidently intended by the designer of the north-east chapel, the church has that rare thing on the Cotswolds, a spire. We have arrived almost at the north porch; on our left, and in front, is the Perpendicular north aisle, rebuilt *c.* 1500, keeping its narrow Norman width. On the north-east corner facing down the path, is an image niche set on the diagonal with a large carved quatrefoil in the plinth, and an ogee pinnacled and crocketed canopy. Above is a huge bearded head and hands holding a scourge (cf. Fairford and Lechlade). Above that is a pinnacle. This is really very elaborate. There is also a continuous parapet below which there is a string-course, with a series of very large grotesques, many yelling their heads off, and including, remarkably, a beakhead grasping a piece of roll-moulding, a Perpendicular copy of the Norman fashion? There are flat buttresses with crocketed finials against the wall below the string-course. The windows have straight heads, with carved rosettes in the spandrels of the arched lights, which have tracery consisting of two-light cinquefoiled heads and a horizontal quatrefoil above, with bowtell mouldings, and deeply hollowed concave casement mouldings. What can be the reason for such a display, we wonder?

Inside it seems it must have been a chantry chapel dedicated to St Katherine. The arms of the Abbot of Oseney appears in the heraldry, and this parish, being of course, part of the Peculiar of Bibury, belonged to Oseney. St Katherine's wheel is carved on the pedestal of her empty niche. There are other Perpendicular features; a simple clerestory on both sides (though not visible on the north externally, owing to the aisle roof), the west tower and spire and the north and south porches. The north porch has a stone rib-vault, a holy water stoup, and on the east an altar niche with a pierced stone cresset to hold lights and a narrow flue for the smoke, perhaps a poor man's chantry, and a stone bench opposite. When you add two original doors, it makes a very interesting countrified late Perpendicular porch. The south porch is like a smaller edition of the other, with its rib-vault and four-centred arched doorway. Otherwise the south side is comparatively plain.

The Norman arcade of three bays survives, with round piers, scalloped capitals and octagonal abaci, supporting pointed arches presumably rebuilt at the same time as the aisle. It cannot be supposed, however, that the rest of the interior is really very pleasing. The flat ceiling of the nave is all right, and the yellow-stained early nineteenth-century pews, with their rather meagre poppy heads, may retain a certain atmosphere of past days, however uncomfortable to sit in; what really jars is the nineteenth-century chancel complete with choir stalls, low Tractarian screen, iron-work and organ. A brave attempt has been made to lighten the reredos by gilding it; but that is not enough, with such insufferably depressing stained glass in the east window.

In the tower is a great rarity: a complete set of three fifteenth-century bells, formerly a 'ring' but now hung as a 'chime'. The bells were cast at Gloucester, probably by Robert Hendley or his successor, and are dedicated to St John the Baptist, St Mary Magdalene and St Mary, Mother of God. A sanctus bell of similar date has been recast.

EASTLEACH

There are two churches here close together. The explanation is that there were two different manors held by different Lords.

Eastleach Martin or Bouthrop was founded by a Norman called Fitzpons, whose son gave it in *c*. 1144 to the Priory of Malvern, together with the hamlet of Cote. This is now the lesser of the two churches in that it is less used and is on the border line of redundancy. It contains, however, some of the best examples of Decorated work in the Cotswolds, because the north transept has beautiful early fourteenth-century Decorated windows, and the spacious chancel remodelled in the thirteenth century has triple lancets tending to the earliest Decorated manner, set under a wide rerearch. The north and south chancel windows are of the same period. The south window of the nave is thirteenth century, *c*. 1270–80, with plain, uncusped intersecting mullions. Work of this period and calibre is comparatively rare; but there are also the more usual Norman and Perpendicular features with a plain Norman south doorway and a splendid Perpendicular west window of three ogee-headed lights with tracery above all in a deep hollow chamfer.

The most appealing thing about the church is its atmosphere, and ancient fittings, and these are precious vulnerable assets which must be safe-guarded, as indeed they seem to be at present. To mention just two of them – there is a rare survival of medieval oak benches and seventeenth-century pews, and the lighting is by oil lamps.

The other church, which is the usual place of worship, Eastleach Turville, or St Andrew, is even more beautiful inside. The manor belonged to the de Lacys till the thirteenth century, and this may explain the south doorway. This Norman south doorway is in the same vibrant style as the Quenington doorways though not so elaborate, and Quenington also was de Lacy property. The whole composition is all of one piece (like the Coronation of the Virgin at Quenington) and the enriched chevron mouldings continue up the jambs and round the tympanum, which has a beautiful carving of Christ in Majesty with a Vesica supported by angels. This work should be added to the Quenington 'school' and dated in the third quarter of the twelfth century. The shafts have scalloped capitals and abaci with round pellet ornament. The hood-mould is billeted.

The interior of the church is striking because of the spacious and beautiful Early English chancel. The north aisle and a north chantry chapel have both disappeared, though the transept survives, and has a fourteenth-century tomb hidden behind the organ.

The Keble family were lords of the manor in the sixteenth century and in 1815 John Keble, author of *The Christian Year*, became curate. He was also in charge of the other church, and the flat stone bridge over the river between the two churches is called Keble's bridge to this day.

One of two medieval bells in Eastleach Martin tower was cast at the Wokingham foundry in the fourteenth century; the maker of the other has not been identified; the saunce is dated 1616; the treble is by Abel Rudhall, 1739.

SOUTHROP

This most precious church is situated in the farmyard of Southrop manor. It is precious because of its age, font, and association with John Keble.

The manor belonged to the same family as the manor of Farmington until 1352. The church is on the site of a Saxon church; but the herring-bone masonry is considered to be post-Conquest and there is quite a lot of it. In the thirteenth century the church was given to the Knights Hospitaller of St John of Jerusalem, Clerkenwell, London.

The Norman north doorway is on quite a grand scale for a small church and would seem to be of the third quarter of the twelfth century or later. The tympanum is decorated with diaper pattern, the jamb shafts have voluted capitals, and the archway has roll moulding and billet ornament. The Norman chancel arch is unmoulded; on the imposts are bands of simple decoration. A later but interesting feature is the aumbrey left high above the arch, a relic of the former rood loft.

The greatest treasure is, of course, the famous font which Zarnecki suggests is dated *c.* 1180. It came from the same workshop as the one at Stanton Fitzwarren. There are eight arches with five Virtues, the others being Moses, Ecclesia and the Synagogue. In the spandrels of the arches are the mansions of the New Jerusalem. After Malmesbury the sculptures look lifeless, though they have great decorative merits, and a far greater iconographical sophistication than most contemporary fonts. The Virtues trample on their opposite vices; Patience on Ira (wrath), Modestia on Ebrietas (excess), Misericordia (pity) on Invidia (envy), Temperancia on Luxuria, Largitas on Avaricia. The font was discovered built into the south doorway by John Keble. Does this indicate Tractarian interest in archaeology? Keble lived in the old Vicarage 1823–25, and there sowed the seeds of the Oxford Movement with Wilberforce, Isaac Williams and Hurrell Froude.

LECHLADE

This church was completely rebuilt in the fifteenth century, so it is all of one piece except that there were alterations fairly soon afterwards, in the beginning of the sixteenth century. Its Perpendicular style is not the same brand as Northleach and Campden and it has its own individuality. It has, however, the usual Perpendicular plan, and in some respects, particularly in the use of plenty of grotesque sculptures and gargoyles, it is like its neighbour Fairford. The date given for the building of Lechlade church is 1470–76.

The Priory of St John at Lechlade was suppressed in 1473 and so it could not have in any way been responsible for rebuilding the parish church, which must as usual have been financed by the wool merchants, in fact the brass of one such, described as 'merchant and woolman of this place', survives. Furthermore, the patronage of the living had devolved on Cecily Duchesss of York in *c.* 1460, and she later obtained a licence to apply the revenues of the Priory to the foundation of three chantries in the parish church.

The church is built of dressed freestone from Taynton. Many Perpendicular towers were intended to carry spires; in this case it was eventually achieved (the 'pratie pyramis of stone' mentioned by Leland *c.* 1540), a rare event in the Cotswolds, but not so rare in Oxfordshire. It has an embattled parapet with pinnacles, and strong diagonal buttresses. Round the spire itself is a band of ornamental quatrefoils. The west doorway has two concave mouldings divided by a roll, and the window above has three lights with straight-forward Perpendicular tracery. The aisle windows, however, are different. They have pointed arches and curiously old-fashioned flowing tracery, rather attractive but not strictly 'Perpendicular' at all, although there is a hollow moulding round the jambs and the mullions are ogee in section. The aisles have solid parapets, like the tower, with pinnacles.

Inside, the arcades also have pointed arches, supported on lozenge-shaped piers with rolls on the edges separated by serpentine mould-ings, which are not reflected in the capitals. These, in fact, are quite straight edged without any suggestion of the concave. The chancel roof is enriched with carved wooden bosses with angels carrying the instruments of the Passion, and supported on stone corbels represent-ing the four Evangelistic symbols and the four Latin fathers of the early church.

It is supposed there was a fire in 1510, and soon afterwards altera-tions and additions were made, which included the building of the spire, the west window and doorway, the large East window in the chancel, the clerestory and the north porch. The East window has a very flat arch with five ogee-headed lights with cinquefoils and a transom with mouchette tracery. Above is a pierced parapet with quatrefoils, and on the north, as at Fairford, a small sacristy with a pierced parapet. The clerestory has straight-headed windows – there is no window over the chancel arch – and a parapet with battle-ments. The north porch looks decidedly Tudor. It has a four-centred arched entrance with almost a horse-shoe twist, and carvings in the spandrels representing a lion and a rose. The ceiling is a flat stone vault with a geometrical pattern of ribs culminating in a small central boss. The manor by now belonged to Katherine of Aragon, and there is a carving on the oak door leading into the sacristy, which resembles her pomegranate badge.

> *Here could I hope . . .*
> *. . .that death did hide from human sight*
> *sweet secrets . . .*

wrote Shelley on a summer evening in Lechlade churchyard in 1815.

THE WINDRUSH VALLEY

Cutsdean, Temple Guiting, Guiting Power, Naunton,
Bourton-on-the-Water, Windrush, Great Barrington,
Little Barrington, Taynton, Burford, Westwell, Holwell,
Fulbrook, Swinbrook, Widford, Asthall, Minster Lovell

The Windrush, which becomes so civilized as it approaches Oxford, begins life in that expanse of woldland known as the North Cotswolds. The fields are large and sometimes featureless. A village like Cutsdean is so exposed, the stone darkens into invisibility when drenched with rain, a place of wild seclusion and disregarded time. In its course the Windrush bore the golden building stone for Windsor and London; but we must leave it at Minster Lovell, with only an admiring glance towards Stanton Harcourt.

CUTSDEAN

The church is situated in a farmyard. There is an ashlar tower with battlements, otherwise it is rather poor nineteenth-century work.

TEMPLE GUITING

The preceptory of the Templars at Guiting was founded about the middle of the twelfth century. It was a cell of the head house of the Templars in London, and was established principally for the sake of managing the property of the Order. The Community consisted of some serving brethren, a chaplain, and one or more Knights under the rule of the preceptor who was always a Knight. There are some remains of the church of this period, notably the corbel table of grotesque heads round the chancel; but the church has too often been the victim of fashionable improvements and the changing tastes of well-intentioned restorers.

From the outside we are struck by the large and somewhat clumsy appearance of the west tower which seems too coarse to be true Perpendicular. The plinth mouldings are Perpendicular in style but very large, as are the diagonal buttresses which end uncomfortably close to the gargoyled string-course below the embattled and fat pinnacles. The explanation is that it is very late, in fact seventeenth century. The nave, however, is true Perpendicular of the fifteenth century with four-centred arched windows, though the four western-most have had Georgian glass inserted into them thus losing their tracery. The effect is endearing in the extreme. There is a Perpendicular embattled parapet and flat roof.

The chancel has evidently been slightly lengthened in the thirteenth century. In the early fourteenth century a small window was set low in the east part of the south wall of the nave, decorated with ball-flower and having stops apparently in the form of jesters' heads. In the north chapel or transept there is also a piscina of this date with ballflower ornament.

The interior is disappointing because of the awful restoration in 1884 when the walls were scraped, and then and since then, anything possible seems to have been done to eradicate the Georgian restoration of the Rev. the Hon. George Talbot who died in 1785. Evidence of the beautiful Georgian work can still be found mouldering under the tower where there is a finely carved classical reredos, Commandment Boards, Creed and Lord's Prayer, and two hatchments. It is a shame that there seems to be no desire or money to save these minor works of art. On the bright side, however, other furnishings of Mr Talbot's time survive in the church, notably the beautiful plaster Royal Arms of George 11 by John Switzer, and the splendid oak pulpit inlaid with sunray and richly carved. There is also a Venetian window in the north chapel, and Mr Talbot's monument by Thomas Scheemakers which states that 'This fabric was substantially repaired and beautified at his sole expense.'

Mention must also be made of the three good panels of late fifteenth-century glass with the Virgin, St James the Less, and St Mary Magdalene; and also the clock dial, 1870, lozenge shaped, gold on black, on the north face of the tower.

GUITING POWER

A distinctly mucked-about church, now cruciform with a west Perpendicular tower, which is dumpy, with bell openings inartistically divided in the middle by mullions, diagonal buttresses, and a west window with grid tracery. The transepts are nineteenth century, in spite of their convincingly good Perpendicular windows; perhaps these have been moved or are reconstructions, certainly the Norman south doorway has been moved to its present position.

The interior is disappointing, with bad glass in the east lancets, very shiny tiles, and scraped walls.

NAUNTON

The first impression of Naunton church is perhaps deceiving because the nave windows have straight heads and round-headed lights which give the impression of being Tudor; but on second thoughts it would seem that Daubeny[1] is right when he says the walls were 'rebuilt from the foundations at the Perpendicular reconstruction of the church, and the windows since robbed of every particle of tracery'. I would therefore now add Naunton to the list of Perpendicular 'wool' churches.

There does not appear to be any documentary evidence for a church at Naunton before 1255. In 1286 the rector was granted permission to undertake a pilgrimage to the Holy Land.[2] There are, however, hardly any remains of a church even of this date; but of Perpendicular features there are some very good examples, notably the pulpit and tower. The tower is characteristic of the district in the fifteenth century, with its embattled parapet, crocketed pinnacles, and gargoyles, beautifully built with moulded plinth, and in ashlar like the rest of the church. The west window is Perpendicular with many vertical mullions, hollow chamfers and grotesque label stops; the belfry openings have two pointed lights, hollow chamfered jambs, and label stops carved as human heads. The eastern-most window in the north aisle is square headed of three Perpendicular lights with tracery similar to that on the pulpit. The other windows are divided by buttresses on the south, and have lost their tracery; and the east window is apparently nineteenth century, though it may be a copy, and it has a slightly Northleach flavour in its freedom.

The pulpit is Naunton's great treasure, stone-carved and of the fifteenth century, richly decorated with canopied panels, pinnacled buttresses and tracery, in many ways similar to the one at Chedworth except that it has lost its pedestal. The font is also fifteenth century, like the one at Guiting Power.

There is a small brass tablet put up by a former rector who is well-known to students of the seventeenth century, Clement Barksdale (1609–87), Librarian of Gloucester Cathedral, favourite chaplain of Lord Chandos of Sudeley, and author of many poems, notably a book called *The Cotswold Muse*. The inscription is translated, 'Clement Barksdale, MA, minister of the Gospel, praying daily, dying daily, exhorts the traveller to meditate upon the Heavenly Kingdom. Sept. 23. 1670. Aged 61.'

There is a saunce by Abel Rudhall, 1741, and a ring of three bells, the two smallest by Thomas Rudhall, 1771; the tenor by Richard Keene, 1684. (c.f. Longborough.)

References

1 Ulric Daubeny, *Ancient Cotswold Churches,* 1921.
2 *Ibid*

BOURTON-ON-THE-WATER

The only church in the Cotswolds with an eighteenth-century classical tower, which was built in *c.* 1784, by a local man called William Marshall. The lower stage is faced in horizontally grooved ashlar upon which stand Ionic pilasters clasping the corners through two stages and supporting a cornice with balustrade and urns. It is crowned by a lead-covered dome.

The rest of the church is all Sir T. G. Jackson's Gothic. First we enter through a Perpendicular south porch. This must be Jackson's way of complimenting the fifteenth-century Cotswold churches, and he must have enjoyed giving it that ogee arch and such big cusps, all of which were the subject of a Royal Academy drawing in 1890. Generally, however, the style is Decorated and in keeping with the medieval chancel, which has a new roof beautifully painted in 1928 by F. E. Howard, who also designed the reredos, and oak screen and rood. All the glass except one window, is by Kempe or Tower which makes it rather dark, and we can hardly see the splendid timber roof of the nave.

In the churchyard there are several excellently carved table-tombs and headstones, particularly one of the name of Jordan with figures and heraldry. The Jordans' monuments appear again farther down stream in the church at Fulbrook.

A modern ring of eight bells by John Taylor and Company.

WINDRUSH

In many ways this is the most perfectly typical Cotswold church imaginable. It has all the necessary ingredients; a beautiful setting on the side of the Windrush valley, with lovely views over Barrington Park, a churchyard with splendidly baroque table tombs made from the finest quality stone quarried near by, a Norman doorway carved with two complete orders of beakhead of the rare bird variety, a Decorated transept, a Perpendicular 'wool' tower, and restorations by Woodyer for Tractarian clergy. In spite of all this, it has that upland feeling, and however lush the spring, we know the cold winds do blow, leaving a bleakness which never quite departs.

The doorway, on the south, dates from the third quarter of the twelfth century, and is therefore miraculously 800 years old. Beakheads round the inner arch and jambs are continuous, though each one is a separate stone or voussoir, the outer arch is the same and the beaks clasp the attached shafts; all except four or five are bird-heads with almond eyes, the ultimate in this form of decoration. The abaci have palmettes. On this side there is a typically narrow south aisle of Norman date, but given a Perpendicular parapet and straight-headed windows in the fifteenth century. The south transept has a window with reticulated tracery; inside it has a piscina with a many-cusped arch, and so it was a chapel in the early fourteenth century. The north wall would be just right for wall-paintings, being tall, with sparse Perpendicular windows with hollow chamfers, rather high up (like Bledington, but not so grand). The tower window or belfry openings have a central mullion, unhappily dividing the arch in the apex.

A ring of six bells; tenor by Messrs Warner, 1863; the others by Abraham Rudhall 1, 1707; also a saunce of 1846.

GREAT BARRINGTON

This was the larger and richer of the two Barringtons, and therefore as one would expect, has a bigger church. Even so, the size of the chancel arch, considering it is Norman, comes as quite a surprise. The chancel was entirely rebuilt during the restoration by F. C. Penrose in 1880 and apart from the family monuments (Countess Talbot by Nollekens) is of no interest. Here we feel the presence of the great house we cannot see.

The nave, however, is a different matter altogether. It has a thirteenth-century north arcade which represents the first remodelling of what must always have been a considerable church. The second remodelling was late Perpendicular *c.* 1511, when the great numbers of Perpendicular square-headed windows were introduced together with a clerestory, making the church beautifully light. The almost flat ceiling of the nave appears contemporary, with its carved bosses. The windows are dull Perpendicular without the relief of interesting tracery.

As we are leaving the church by the north door, we realize there is an interesting monument worthy of more attention. An angel is helping two children dressed in their everyday clothes to walk on the clouds. It is thought to be designed by Francis Bird and carved by Christopher Cass. Both children died of the smallpox, she 'at her aunt Catchmay's in Gloucester' in 1711 in her eighth year, and he at the Royal Academy at Angers in France in his fifteenth year in 1720. 'I say unto you that in heaven their angels do always behold the Face of my Father which is in heaven.'

A complete ring of six bells by Abraham Rudhall II, 1733. (c.f. Colesbourne.)

LITTLE BARRINGTON

This small village on the Windrush, in close proximity to the quarries which provided the best stone for so many buildings of our national heritage, is now at least half inhabited by week-enders. The church, which is by no means central, and is, in fact, in a side road, is approached down a path, down steps into the porch and down again into the nave. The porch has the usual niche on the east, and stone seats either side east and west. The Norman south doorway is very satisfactory; it is late twelfth century and has keeled shafts with stiff-leaf capitals transitional to Early English. The arch has three orders deeply cut with chevron and lozenge and splendid dogtooth on the hood-mould, all quite well preserved. On the north, however, is the big surprise, a carved tympanum of a Majesty and angels with extended wings, also quite well preserved but not *in situ* and not protected. The west end of the north aisle has the tower, and a Perpendicular plinth runs half way along the aisle wall. There is a smart Perpendicular window with deep dripmould stops and fine ashlar work. The east end of the aisle is built of rubble but the east window is good Perpendicular. Here then we have a church not unlike Aldsworth in plan, with a Norman north arcade with round piers and scalloped capitals, though here the original round Norman arches survived the remodelling of the aisle. It was formed into a Perpendicular chapel complete with image niches either side of the east window, one one side for the Virgin and two the other for St Peter and St Paul. Alas, they have long now been empty. Note also the red letter text on the north wall. Both chancel and nave have very nice wagon roofs. In spite of all this interest the interior slightly fails to please, though I am always delighted to see a *corona lucis* still hanging where the Victorians left it. The east window, 1888, is a poor trade job and the two windows in the chancel south wall are a genteel pair, early twentieth century.

The churchyard is a delight; though simple and without large numbers of table tombs and cherub heads, it is a worthy member of the Cotswold group of churchyards which excel all others in England. For instance, just to the east of the south porch there is a table tomb with a flat top and gadrooned edge, of Joseph and Ursula Beauchamp. 1726. What could be nicer?

A sanctus bell in an open cote above the gable over the chancel arch. In the tower, a ring of three bells; treble, an early example of Henry Neale's work dated 1638; second by Edward Neale, 1659; tenor by John Rudhall, 1832.

TAYNTON

As this is the place from whence the stone came to build so many Perpendicular churches, we expect to see something more remarkable in this line. However, after a few minutes' reflection we realize that this is a church with considerable charm. The tower itself perhaps, is not one of which to boast grandiloquently; but it is quite tall, has an embattled parapet with gargoyles, and is not unlike the one at Bibury; there are also a Perpendicular clerestory with straight-headed windows, and big mullioned and transomed windows in the south aisle. The best work, however, belongs to a slightly earlier date when the windows had more flamboyant tracery and ballflower decoration was used. The north aisle is like this and is said to be *c*. 1360. In both nave and aisles are excellent stone corbels carved as heads.

BURFORD

The wealth of medieval Burford came of course from the wool trade, and one of the earliest merchants' guilds was established here between 1088 and 1107. About 1400 it was described with Northleach as one of the leading wool-markets in the Cotswolds. It reached its peak in the fifteenth century and early sixteenth, and in the reign of Edward vi it was 'a very great market town'.

The church is a complicated building which has developed in a curious way from the Norman, of which only the central tower and the west wall of the nave remain. 'The gradual enlargement', writes Jennifer Sherwood, 'has produced a cluster of aisles and chapels and a complex labyrinthine interior with the parts at odd angles and on different levels'.

The remodelling in the fifteenth century, when the town was at its peak, was widespread, and almost all the windows are of this date. The funds came from the wool-merchants; but the exact donors and dates are unknown. The medieval tombs have been defaced and most inscriptions and brasses lost. One to John Spycer, who died in 1437, survives and that of his wife. They gave a rood loft and a gable window to the church, perhaps that in St Thomas's Chapel. Work began with the nave which has normal Perpendicular arcades with quatrefoil piers, that is, alternately concave and rolled. A big concave moulding surrounds each pointed arch, but the capitals are not markedly concave. The hood-moulds have head-stops in the costume of *c.* 1420, and the hoods on the windows in the clerestory are similar, and those in the north aisle, apparently all by one mason.

Against the eastern respond of the north arcade there survives a wooden chantry chapel, coloured and enchanting. After the supression of chantries this chapel survived because it was used as a pew by the occupants of The Priory. The other great Perpendicular feature is the porch which has a fan-vault, rather like the one in the Wilcote Chapel at North Leigh, and these two are supposed to be the only fan-vaults in the county outside Oxford itself. They both have designs of four quatrefoils between the fans. The porch walls internally are panelled with four-centred arches having central mullions. Externally the front is a grid broken by three canopied image niches. The date is said to be *c.* 1450. Although several features remind us of Northleach and Cirencester porches, we also feel the nearness of Oxford.

In the north chapel there is a large canopied monument by the Southwark school of sculptors to the Lord Chief Justice Tanfield. At the foot is the kneeling effigy of his grandson the famous Lucius Cary, Viscount Falkland, who is credited with the epigrammatic remark: 'When it is not necessary to change it is necessary not to change'. He was killed fighting for the King in 1643.

A ring of eight bells, tenor (largest) a fine medieval bell of a rare type by an unidentified fourteenth-century founder; two by Henry Neale, of Burford, 1635; two by the Bonds of Burford, 1868, and 1885; one by Matthew Bagley, 1771 : and two by Gillett and Johnston,

1950. In addition are a saunce by Abraham Rudhall 11, 1720, and two more bells by Henry Neale, 1635, removed from the tower in 1950 and preserved in the church.

WESTWELL

The church is set on a slight elevation next a large Georgian former rectory, and above the duck pond and green. Other gentlemen's houses are grouped round with barns and cottages. The churchyard is more than up to Cotswold standard, with excellently carved headstones, and table tombs, including one (John Large died 1781) which looks almost like an inverted pyramid, anyway of some strange classical derivation.

The church was enlarged one bay to the west in 1869 when the wooden bell turret was built, otherwise most of the Victorian alterations have been undone and the church now has a very nice stone floor. We enter through the south porch, which is fourteenth century; on its east wall is an ogee-headed image niche or altar with trefoiled arch and embattled cornice (some say it is the re-used piscina; but that is not proven) in the usual position for such things when porches were used for marriage contracts, and the rest. The doorway is Norman with zigzag order, the chancel arch Transitional, the outer order on shafts with scalloped and cushion capitals, the abaci carved with star-in-square pattern. However, the most unusual feature for the Cotswolds is the circular cinquefoiled or rose east window, which is thought to be of Transitional date, now filled with good and admirably clear stained glass by Clayton and Bell. The chancel otherwise has Early English lancet windows. The living belonged to the Knights Hospitaller of near-by Quenington.

In the nave, east of the porch, there is an important straight-headed Perpendicular window, certainly important to the donors. The few fragments of original glass are tantalizing, as they show a Crucifixion, the head, shoulders and legs of Christ, the heads of the Virgin and St John, and a group of five donors. The date was 1522, and the donors were copyholders who farmed the ancient tenancies of the manor, and had done well out of their sheep. The one lady, Isabel Grelle, is clearly visible wearing the gabled head-dress of the time of Henry VIII.

After the Reformation the rectors were often professors of Christ Church, Oxford. Richard Thorneton is the one who died in 1614 and has a recumbent effigy by the altar. The nineteenth-century

Rev. J. E. Bode wrote the famous hymn 'O Jesus, I have promised to serve Thee to the end.'

There is another intriguing monument to one Charles Trinder, of a persistent Cotswold surname. He was a yeoman's son who worked for the Heylyn family of Burford and married his master's daughter. His own daughters, in their turn, married into the local squire families, like the Sackvilles at Bibury. This seventeenth-century monument has rustic carving of great charm in a baroque frame of two pairs of twisted columns and a scroll pediment enclosing swags and a coat of arms, the head and base of which have grotesque heads quite Gothic in feeling.

The organ is a Henry Willis.

HOLWELL

A small Victorian church near the zoo at Bradwell Grove, built in 1895 for a gentleman who had made a fortune in umbrella frames, it is rather a heavy-handed interpretation of the Cotswold brand of Gothic, by a Banbury architect, W. E. Mills. The sanctuary has windows by Bryans and an 'English Altar'.

Two bells by Mears, one dated 1847, the other 1856.

FULBROOK

The Early English porch is distinctly impressive, with an outer arch and three inner orders. Inside, the north arcade is Transitional, of four bays with round piers and trumpet-scalloped capitals. The chancel arch is Early English, but round with fine roll mouldings and shafts with bell capitals. The nave has an added clerestory with small straight-headed Perpendicular windows. Altogether these and other medieval features make this a charming and unusual little church. Next to the Jordan tablet on the north of the chancel, there is one in the manner of Christoper Kempster with cherubs and carving, 1695.

SWINBROOK

To appreciate this remarkable church we must know that Swinbrook was the home of a now extinct family called Fettiplace. Their mansion was south of the church, and was built in 1490; but it was demolished when the last Fettiplace died in 1805.

The Perpendicular east window of the chancel is of the grid pattern, large and restored, and now filled with clear glass coming down low it floods with light the remarkable Fettiplace monuments.

These consist of two fascinating trios of reclining gentlemen, one lot Tudor, the other Stuart. The first was prepared by Sir Edmund Fettiplace, who died in 1613, for his grandfather, father and himself, the second by Sir Edmund, who died in 1686, for his great-uncle, his father and himself. Compare the rigid Tudor style with the more realistic Stuart, and also the fashions in hirsuteness. The earlier one has primitive classical surrounds like some in Burford and must be local work. The later is signed by William Byrd, an Oxford sculptor, and is in marble and alabaster. There are also brasses in the chancel, and a monument by James Annis of London to Sir George Fettiplace, Bart., who died in 1743, not unworthy of Rysbrack. Monuments are even placed on the cylindrical piers of the arcade with total disregard for the architecture; but in this case they get away with it.

The sanctuary has very nice communion rails with turned balusters, and there are stalls with misericords probably from Burford Priory.

In the east window of the south aisle there are fragments of medieval glass collected after a German land mine exploded in the village on 26 September 1940 and blew the east window out.

Just outside in the churchyard is the grave of Unity Mitford, the misguided friend of Hitler.

WIDFORD

The small church stands by itself in a field just across the Windrush. It has great charm : unspoiled and unsophisticated, preserving its eighteenth-century feeling, and barn-like appearance.

Inside, the floors are stone-flagged, and the walls lime-washed, except where there are wall-paintings. The Communion rails are flat balusters; there are box-pews, and the pulpit is more or less matched by a reading desk on the other side of the chancel arch. Above them are the Commandment Boards.

Built on the site of a Roman villa, a fragment of mosaic pavement is exposed *in situ* in the chancel.

ASTHALL

The church is approached on the north and we notice a fine baroque table tomb with finials, and other extravagantly carved headstones as we walk to the porch. To the west overlooking the churchyard stands the many-gabled manor house, childhood home of Nancy Mitford and her sisters.

The Norman arcade divides the north aisle and nave almost exactly. It is *c.* 1160 or later, and has cylindrical piers with very large flat scalloped capitals like some others upstream, Little Rissington and Farmington. The arches are pointed. The chancel arch appears to be Victorian Norman and has beakheads clasping roll mouldings, though they are too unnaturally spread out to look original; perhaps there were some there before. There are also beakhead corbels in the north aisle roof. The nave roof has winged-angel corbels.

The walls are mostly scraped; but the chancel has Victorian wall-painting.

In the fourteenth century the north transept was remodelled so that it towers above the nave, and contains a tomb recess of gigantic proportions; but the stone effigy of the Lady is delicately carved and she gathers her robe up under her arm. In this transept the altar is peculiar as it has a piscina attached, and there are rare remains of fourteenth-century glass.

MINSTER LOVELL

Entirely rebuilt by William Lord Lovell *c.* 1450. Here we have a church all of one piece, next the ruins of an exactly contemporary house, set in the unspoiled Windrush valley still lush and pastoral with grazing cows in the water-meadows. The church is cruciform and quite elaborate, with nave, chancel and transepts. The crossing has composite piers with concave mouldings which are not followed in the capitals, alternating with round mouldings. The piers are free standing and there are vaulted passages behind each, as well as a good stone fan-vault under the tower with moulded ribs and bosses. It is all Perpendicular and marvellous in spite of the walls being scraped; even the pews look contemporary, and there are fragments of original stained glass in the tracery. The big east and west windows are of the grid pattern more usual in the London–Oxford area than in the Cotswolds. They have five lights with cinquefoiled heads, pointed (not four-centred) arches, and central divisions, but all neat and refined. There is a niche on the east wall of the big north porch, and also an image bracket. The doorway has a roll or bowtell moulding. The chancel windows also have round or bowtell mouldings. Lord Lovell who died in 1455 has a splendid alabaster effigy in the south transept.

TRIBUTARIES OF THE WINDRUSH

The Dikler

*Lower Swell, Upper Swell, Wyck Rissington, Little
Rissington, Great Rissington*

The Eye

Upper Slaughter, Lower Slaughter

The Sherborne Brook

Farmington, Sherborne

The Windrush has tributaries called Dikler and Eye. The Dikler
rises north-west of Stow in the lakes at Donnington and flows south.
On its banks are the Swells. The Eye waters the Slaughters. In 1294
Edmund Earl of Cornwall gave to the abbot of Hailes 40 acres of
pasture in Lower Swell.

LOWER SWELL, ST MARY

The entrance is into the south aisle, which was the original Norman
church. The main part of the church now is a Victorian addition. It
is well looked after, and having been redecorated in 1972 the
whitened walls are fresh and clean, and a good background for
flower arrangements. Everywhere there are Clayton & Bell windows
and in the chancel mural paintings by the same firm showing the
Passion of Our Lord, with typical decorations of the 1880's like pots
of aesthetic flowers; the last mural had to be obliterated because the
wall was so damp there was little left. The existence of this part of
the church, designed in 1852 by J. C. Buckler who dreamed and
drew fine things but realized rather poor ones, is due to a remarkable
incumbent, David Royce.

Royce was a typical example of a late nineteenth-century country
parson with a passion for antiquarian pursuits. Born in Rutland, he
took a BA degree at Christchurch, Oxford, in 1840, became rector
of Lower Swell in 1850 and remained till his death in 1902. He
assisted Canon Greenwell during his excavations of barrows in the
Cotswolds, 1875-6, and kept the finds, now in the Royce Collection
at Bristol Museum. In 1876 he was a founder member of the Bristol
& Gloucestershire Archaeological Society. His collection contains
4,500 flint arrowheads, nearly all from a few square miles west of
Stow-on-the-Wold.

Afterwards came the Fenwicks, who got Lutyens to build a house for them, and so the War Memorial at the crossroads in the village is by Lutyens.

An earlier resident was Sir Robert Atkyns, who complained in 1683 how badly the church was kept up. However, considerable Norman detail has survived through the ages. The original chancel arch has an outer order with carved stones showing animals and such like, and the capitals on the north jamb also have little figures which must have pleased the medieval mind. The tympanum over the entrance door is also carved, with a branching tree of life and a dove pecking a branch.

UPPER SWELL

This is a very pretty hamlet on the river Dikler, shielded by hills and trees. The house next the church looks derelict, and the church is threatened with redundancy. Both these facts should only be transitory.

The church is charming with ashlar nave, bellcote, and a very good Perpendicular window in the same position in the south nave wall as the one at Condicote, but even better preserved. The west window is also Perpendicular, with a two-centred arch with hollow moulding. There is a Norman south doorway, through which we enter and find a stone floor, whitened walls, Perpendicular font and eighteenth-century pulpit.

The organ (1872) is by Nicholson & Co.

WYCK RISSINGTON

The church is uniquely interesting for its beautiful thirteenth-century chancel, with the incunabula of tracery in its east wall. The tower is also splendidly massive and of the same date. The monks of Eynsham Abbey, near Oxford, are probably responsible for building this enchanting chancel, and the tower. The chancel is lit at the east by two pairs of tall lancets surmounted by concave lozenge-shaped lights, and near the apex of the gable is a plain lozenge-shaped light. Both externally and internally they are drawn into a coherent design by continuous string-courses. Two lancets with a concave-sided lozenge are also found at Langford, not very far away across the Oxfordshire border. The chancel is quite spacious with several aumbries, piscinas and recesses, and stone benches for the priests. The only obtrusion is the organ, now famous since Gustav Holst was organist here. So we must forgive it, and the fact that such a delightful composer played here greatly adds to the romance.

The rest of the church was, frankly, much spoiled by the restorer J. E. K. Cutts, who added a north aisle and put in the shiny tiles. There are, however, Perpendicular windows of grid type in the south wall of the nave, and there is some medieval glass of the Crucifixion with sun, moon and stars.

LITTLE RISSINGTON

From the outside this church looks really dull, and we have to walk along a path across a field to get to it. We also notice that the churchyard is full of Royal Air Force graves, a stark reminder of the realities of life, far removed from the Cotswold dream to which we are accustomed.

The church belonged to the Abbey of Oseney, and so it ought not to surprise us to find quite a large Early English chancel with lancet windows, three at the east, with glass by Wailes, 1862, and an aumbry not unlike the many such at Bibury. The interior is altogether more interesting with its north arcade of twelfth-century cylindrical piers, large overhanging scalloped capitals, and round arches. The small tower has been curiously inserted into the north-west corner with an octagonal pier to support the flattened arch of the arcade. On the whole, however, over-restoration has removed most of its attraction, and there are excessively shiny tiles on the floor.

GREAT RISSINGTON

A cruciform church of undoubted archaeological interest, it somehow fails to please in spite of the studied harmony of its twentieth-century interior fittings. On the east wall of the rebuilt porch is a late fifteenth-century carved stone panel with an ogee cusped arch and embattled cornice containing a Crucifixion and below, possibly, the Resurrection. The central tower rises from four dissimilar pointed arches of *c.* 1200. The chancel and several other parts were rebuilt in 1873, possibly by Pearson.

In the south transept there is a tiny twentieth-century chantry chapel exactly fitting the medieval piscina.

The organ is correctly placed at the west end below a rose window, which is very dramatic, fully abstract and deep blue in colour. The floors are repaved with stone, and the other windows have clear glass except the east window by Clayton & Bell. Everything is well-considered, including the proportions of the 'English altar'.

UPPER SLAUGHTER

The approach is attractive in a cutting through the churchyard, with cottages by Lutyens on our right. The Perpendicular tower top stage has battlements and pinnacles, but the bottom stage is earlier and has buttresses at right angles. It was inserted into the nave, causing archaeological confusion inside; there are even two Perpendicular fonts. However, the details are interesting: glass by Clayton & Bell, monuments, and an additional mortuary chapel by Benjamin Ferrey in Puginesque style.

The organ (1855) is by J. W. Walker.

LOWER SLAUGHTER

The village is well known for its picturesque qualities. The church is nineteenth century and rather successful as it incorporates the original Transitional arcade of four good bays. It was done by Benjamin Ferrey. His spire now has a fibre-glass top, and you would hardly tell the difference. Inside there are candlesticks like the ones at Farmington, a lovely alabaster reredos, nice glass by Clayton & Bell in the west window of the north aisle; but there is no plaster on the walls.

FARMINGTON

The original Norman church consisted of nave and chancel only, and the Norman corbel table can be seen running almost the entire way round both. It has grotesque heads including at least one beakhead on the south of the nave; but many heads have gone. There is a long range of large ball pellets (c.f. Barnsley chancel arch) and zigzag ornament in low relief, and the Norman masonry of squarish blocks of ashlar is often undisturbed.

A north arcade was added in later Norman times with cylindrical piers with exceptionally large overhanging scalloped capitals, and pointed arches which could be transitional (or are they later?) The Norman chancel arch is very decorative.

The western tower is Perpendicular. The north aisle was rebuilt rather badly in 1890–91.

Most people will remember the tall candlesticks at the end of each pew more than the eighteenth-century pulpit, and the *art nouveau* lectern, though these are very good.

SHERBORNE

The valley of the Sherborne Brook is lusher here than anywhere else because the water has been artificially broadened, and everywhere there are signs of the eighteenth-century lords' mastery over nature. The original Norman church was abandoned, and all that remains is a doorway in a cottage, which can be numbered amongst the few examples of beakhead ornament remaining in the Cotswolds, though the motif is very weathered and only on the jambs.

The existing church has a medieval tower and spire and was rebuilt (next the mansion of the Lords Sherborne), possibly by Salvin in 1841–42, and is really a mausoleum of the Dutton family, with splendid monuments by well-known sculptors, Richard Westmacott, the elder, and J. M. Rysbrack. There is a shrouded effigy by Burman of 1661, and others by Bacon and Theed.

In the tower is a ring of six bells; one of them cast *c.* 1400 by an unidentified founder, two by Henry Bagley III, 1742 and 1746; the remaining three by Edward Neale, 1653; one of them inscribed: *When I was cast into the ground I lost my old tone and revived my sound.*

THE EVENLODE VALLEY

Evenlode, Adlestrop, Oddington, Daylesford

Rising in the north-east corner of the Cotswolds this river marches with the Oxford plain, and cannot by us be pursued into Wychwood Forest, except in drawing attention to the fact that just before it joins the Thames at Cassington, it passes near that most beautiful 'Cotswold Perpendicular' style church at Church Hanborough.

EVENLODE

The interior of this medieval church is more interesting than the exterior, but even so it is colourless and dark in spite of the absence of stained glass. There are some fine features, particularly the arcade of pointed arches without capitals or responds and lozenge-shaped octagonal piers, probably fourteenth century, and the late Norman chancel arch with scalloped capitals.

The rarest of furnishings is here too, a pre-Reformation wooden pulpit, of wine-glass shape and tracery in low relief.

A ring of five bells; two by Henry Bond, 1897; one by John Rudhall, 1831; one by G. Mears, 1858; and the tenor, uninscribed, probably by Henry Bagley whose catalogue, dated 1732, states he cast a ring of five for Evenload (*sic*).

ADLESTROP

This church is rather disappointing, if we are aware of its vague connection with Jane Austen, or are expecting a building by Sanderson Miller. In fact the most Miller-like objects to be seen are the gateposts now supporting a Jubilee iron overthrow at the entrance to the churchyard.

It has been restored several times, and looks thoroughly overrestored; however the walls are whitened and there are hatchments and memorial tablets to the Leigh family, and a pleasant east window by Hardman.

ODDINGTON

The parish church of the Holy Ascension was built in 1852. We can be thankful in one way that was so, because it meant the old church of St Nicholas was not restored and altered by the Victorians of that date. The new church is uninspiring though it has a certain harmony, with windows by Wailes, Clayton & Bell (hidden behind the organ) and Powell; but the east window is early twentieth century and insipid.

The old church is entirely delightful, and has recently staged a considerable 'come-back' in its popularity. The bells have been rehung for ringing, and regular practices take place. The great Doom painting on the north wall has been restored by Prof. and Mrs Baker. The original church is now represented by the south aisle which was the nave, and the tower which is built over what was the chancel of the twelfth-century church. In the thirteenth century, when it belonged to the Archbishop of York, a new, much larger nave and chancel were built on to the north, separated by an arcade. The top stage of the tower was built in the fifteenth century and resembles the top of the tower at Longborough, except that at Oddington the pinnacles are broken off. The nave has a Perpendicular roof and west window with grid tracery and Tudor arch.

Inside the church, with the exception of the Victorian reredos, the eighteenth-century atmosphere prevails, including the William iv arms over the chancel arch, a marvellous tall pulpit of Jacobean origin, richly carved and a good colour, stone flags on the floor, and above all the huge wall-painting of *c*. 1480 covering the entire window-less wall of the nave.

The church is some distance from the village which must have moved; but the churchyard continued to be used for burials as there is a group of good mid-late nineteenth-century headstones with deeply incised lettering.

DAYLESFORD

Another place on the Evenlode river as it wends its way towards Oxford and henceforth passes out of Cotswold country. Although it has been said that this is J. L. Pearson at his worst, we cannot allow the church to be 'written off' by such a prejudiced judgement, and prefer to think that if he had died immediately after designing the church, he might have been thought of as a 'rogue' architect; but he did not, and it represents an interesting phase in his brilliant career. Besides which, it is of such fine material that each detail, and there are many, is as perfectly preserved as when it was built. The composition is dominated by a central tower with a pyramidal spire of unusual outline, and perhaps this is what some cannot forgive. The interior, however, puts it in the forefront of Victorian country churches, a perfect *ensemble* with a stone vaulted sanctuary, wrought iron screens and a marvellous set of Clayton & Bell windows, jewel-like, small-scale medallions of brilliant colour. Alas! There are holes coming in Wailes' east window, and it looks as if the church is hardly ever used.

In the churchyard, east of the church, is Warren Hastings' grave, a Coade-stone monument in neo-Greek taste.

TRIBUTARY OF THE EVENLODE

The Westcote Brook

Icomb, Westcote, Fifield, Idbury, Bledington

ICOMB

The first thing we see is the west tower, apparently Jacobean, with gables east and west, but not on all sides as at Barnsley. The south transept projects to the east side of the porch, and has Perpendicular windows; the Tudor arch of the south window is divided in the centre with a mullion, and the east window has a straight head and quatrefoils in the tracery. The chancel is Early English and has buttresses and lancet windows.

Inside, the church is disappointing as it appears over-restored and rather dark, and there are some awful Victorian tiles. However, the south transept turns out to be the chantry chapel of Sir John Blaket who died in 1431, and there is a splendid tomb, with the effigy of a Knight under a cusped canopy, and resting on a tomb-chest, carved with figures of the Trinity, a Knight and Lady, angels with shields, a female saint and an archangel.

WESTCOTE

This is a mostly rebuilt and architecturally rather uninteresting little building; but obviously used and well cared for.

FIFIELD

Fifield is almost off the edge of the Cotswolds, and it is not really an attractive village though its church is not without interest. It has an unusual fourteenth-century octagonal tower with a small spire with a ball finial. The south porch also is peculiar, in that it has a stone roof carried on one arched transverse rib, quite impressive in a simple way. The rest of the church was mostly rebuilt in the nineteenth century; but it retains a good Perpendicular font, an Early English chancel arch, lancet windows and a Decorated east window in the chancel. In one chancel window, there are some early heraldic glass quarries, including the crown in the thornbush design, in allusion to Henry VII's victory at Bosworth in 1485. The Victorian glass consists of the east window by Wailes, a north window in the nave by O'Connor and a south window by Tower, who succeeded Kempe. The altar is now advanced to a westward position and it all looks a bit awkward.

IDBURY

Again almost off the edge of the Cotswolds, so perhaps it does not matter so much that a heart-shaped polished granite gravestone was allowed to appear in the churchyard in 1974. There is also precedent for unsuitable design and material with the granite Celtic Cross of 1907 supported on flying buttresses like the corona of a church in Aberdeen.

43 Lechlade: *sacristy with parapet pierced by quatrefoils.*

Northleach: top (44) stone vault in porch; bottom (45) image of the Virgin over porch door.

Stained glass. Top: left (46) Buckland east window, late 15th century; right (47) Bagendon, the Virgin, 15th century. Bottom: left (48) Edgeworth, a bishop, 2nd half of 14th century; right (49) Stroud, window in parish church by J. C. N. Bewsey, c. 1913: St George and St Martin.

Monuments. Top: left (50) Sapperton, detail of Poole monument, c. 1616; right (51) Miserden, detail of Sandys monument c. 1640. Bottom (52) Sir William and Lady Sandys.

Pulpits. Top: left (53) Oddington St Nicholas, Jacobean woodwork; right (54) North Cerney, carved stone, c. 1480. Bottom: left (55) Chedworth, another stone pre-Reformation pulpit; right (56) Northleach, stone, goblet-shaped, 15th century.

Screens. Top: left (57) Turkdean, 1949 by Peter Falconer; right (58) Chalford, lectern c. 1930 by Peter van de Waals. Bottom: left (59) Fairford: screens and stalls c. 1500; right (60) Somerford Keynes: chancel screen with quatrefoil piercings, 15th century.

Chest-tombs. Top *(61) Brimpsfield: lyre-console ending in a coil like an Ionic volute, 1717.*
Middle (62) Painswick: cherubs and consoles, 1774. Bottom (63) Painswick: chest-tomb
with lyre-shaped ends, 1739.

Top (64) Winson: a group of chest-tombs with lids which are not unusual in the east Cotswolds.
Bottom (65) Boxwell: Classical chest-tomb, rococo and symbolical.

Top, Daglingworth: left (66) lyre-shaped end with acanthus; right (67) lyre-shaped end with portrait bust, late 17th early 18th century. Middle (68) Bibury: headstone. Bottom (69) Elkstone: chest-tomb c. 1690.

70 Great Barrington: monument to the Bray children c. 1720, perhaps by Francis Bird.

Left (71) Tetbury: Classical chest-tomb with elaborate 'lid'; right (72) Withington: tea-caddy.

73 Windrush: headstone with baroque cartouche and three cherubs.

On the monument inscription:

Sir JOHN DUTTON *Baronet* PETER
Son of Sir RALPH DUTTON by MARY the Daughter of JOHN BARWICK
Doctor of Physick departed this Life February the first 1742/3
in the sixty first Year of His Age
. He was twice Married
First, to MARY, only Child of Sir RUSHOUT CULLEN of *UPTON*
in *WARWICKSHIRE Baronet*, by Her having no Issue
His second Wife was MARY, Daughter of FRANCIS KECK
of Great *TEW*, in the County of *OXFORD Esquire*
By whom He had One Daughter, who dyed an Infant

He represented this County in Parliament
With great Integrity,
Was an excellent Justice of Peace
Hospitable, Affable, and benevolent.

74 *Sherborne: monument by J. M. Rysbrack, 1749.*

75 Tetbury: brass chandelier, 1781.

Hawling: top (76) Perpendicular tower, Georgian alterations; bottom (77) Venetian east window in chancel.

Top, Tetbury St Saviour's: left (78) font by S. W. Daukes, 1848; right (79) Corona lucis gaselier by John Hardman. Bottom: left (80) Miserden: 'English altar' by F. E. Howard, 1928; right (81) Fairford: Lady chapel altar by Geoffrey Webb, c. 1913.

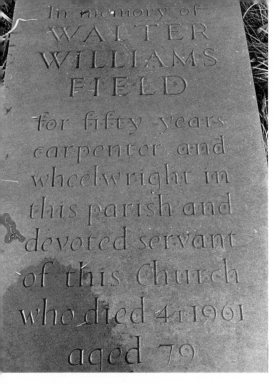

In memory of
WALTER
WILLIAMS
FIELD

for fifty years
carpenter and
wheelwright in
this parish and
devoted servant
of this Church
who died 4.1.1961
aged 79

82 Winson: ledger stone in churchyard by Bryant Fedden, c. 1969.

83 Bibury: headstone by Simon Verity, c. 1971.

In memory of
Robert Charles
Stallard who died
February 1st 1960
Also Sarah Ann
his wife who died
September 13th 1944

The church, however, is of considerable interest and charm. Here again is an exercise in fifteenth-century Perpendicular, which strikes us at once as we approach from the south, and it is the south side which has been given a Perpendicular clerestory with four quite large, rather flat, four-centred arched headed windows and grid tracery, with deep hollow casement moulding and hood-mould stops. The parapet has gargoyles. There is a stone bell turret with pinnacles. On the north side the Perpendicular windows have quatrefoil tracery at the top which is rather unusual, and on this side there is also a Norman doorway.

Inside, the arcade is on the north, with clustered keeled shafts supporting pointed arches with wave-moulding, and is early fourteenth century. The nave has a Perpendicular roof supported on carved corbels. There is an elaborate Perpendicular font.

The woodwork is old; there are old carved bench ends, and a fifteenth-century screen, with simple traceried openings. The windows generally have clear glass. There is a passage squint from the former north aisle chapel.

BLEDINGTON

Farther down the hill from Idbury, but back into Gloucestershire, we come to this extraordinary church, famous for its Perpendicular windows and stained glass. The earliest work is twelfth century and includes the main structure of the nave. The chancel is Early English. In the fifteenth century the church as usual benefited from the wool trade, and the tower was built curiously on three additional arches within the original Norman nave, its west side standing on the west wall of the nave which has a reticulated window. The north wall of the nave has two tiers of windows with straight heads and grid tracery, though the more elaborate have ogee-headed lights and tracery with trefoils which match top and bottom. Part is arranged symmetrically round a doorway with windows above and either side. The Perpendicular windows on the south side also have deep hood-moulds, and some stops carved with human heads. The south aisle west window has a four-centred arch, rather flat, and also the same tracery with trefoils top and bottom, fitting snugly above the ogee headed lights.

The interior must have been gorgeous before the Reformation. Each window has a pedestal set in the concave casement moulding to support an image. These pedestals are treated rather like bowtells, but they are hexagonal or octagonal and have quite concave-sided capitals to support the images. Over each image space is a nodding ogee canopy. Bledington belonged to Winchcombe Abbey, and one can only suppose that this was the sort of thing which went on there.

A recess with a three-light window was built leading from the south-west corner of the chancel into a passage squint to the south aisle and this has always been thought of as a chantry chapel. The glass survives, to a certain extent, as fragments pieced together and in some cases as nearly complete panels. One is dated 1470. They include representations of the Virgin (partly restored) in a blue mantle, holding a rosary in one hand and a sceptre in the other. In the clerestory are St George in fifteenth-century armour and the dragon, and a group of donors; in the chantry chapel window the Coronation of the Virgin, and the sacramental words *priesthood* and *wedlock*. Nearly all the walls show signs of wall-painting.

There are some panelled fifteenth-century bench-ends, not unlike those at Idbury. The simple Holy Table is now preferred to the 'English Altar' previously provided by F. E. Howard.

THE AMPNEY BROOK

Barnsley, Ampney Crucis, Ampney St Mary, Ampney St Peter, Harnhill, Driffield, Poulton, Meysey Hampton, Down Ampney

BARNSLEY

The church tower can be seen for some distance, among the trees, by people coming on the main road from Cirencester. The church is situated on a slight rise on one side of the centre of the long street which is Barnsley village. The Elizabethan tower with its simple gables and finials looks pretty by any standard, and the standard at Barnsley is high. We approach the church from the north side, which is fortunate as it is much more agreeable than the south. The north aisle is Perpendicular with a parapet, and there is also a west window at the bottom of the tower of this date. Tradition and the county historians say these alterations were made by Sir Edmund Tame, who built Rendcomb Church. What has not been destroyed by severe subsequent restorations is Norman. The chancel is built of square Norman freestone blocks, and has a delightful corbel table of grotesque heads, including one beakhead. The rest of the south side is all nineteenth century, including an organ chamber of *c.* 1876, and lancet windows in the nave inserted by J. P. Harrison in the restoration of 1843–47. The restored Perpendicular north porch has a niche in its east wall, and a round Norman doorway into the nave.

The church has lime-washed walls, a stone floor, some nicely lettered ledger stones, and a pointed chancel arch on Norman piers which lean outwards, and are enriched with large pellet-mouldings round the abaci. The nave roof is nineteenth century and is omnipresent, and combined with the severe window openings on the south, and the mass of Willement and Wailes glass, gives the church a distinctly nineteenth-century feeling. This is hardly surprising as the re-introduction of 'medieval' features was Canon Howman's expressed purpose in 1843, when, on coming to Barnsley, he found the classical Georgian interior, complete with round-headed windows and flat plaster ceilings, very distasteful to him.

Items of interest which have survived are the superb Elizabethan Holy Table, the Samuel Green organ, which would be better seen if its pretty façade faced into the chancel, and the 1691 tablet to the wife of Squire Bourchier on the east wall of the north aisle. This aisle was probably the chantry chapel of St Nicholas mentioned in an early sixteenth-century will.[1] It then became the private pew of the manorial family who in the early eighteenth century were called Perrot and employed John James of Greenwich to build Barnsley Park. There are no other monuments, except later tablets to the Wykeham-Musgraves who inherited, because the Perrots were buried at North Leigh, and not here. Canon Howman, an honorary canon of Bristol Cathedral, paid for the Willement glass in the east window in memory of his first wife who was cousin to the Musgraves.

A ring of three bells; treble by Edward Neale, 1677, with Royal Arms as at Cherington; second by John Rudhall, 1828; tenor by Messrs. Warner, 1865.

References

[1] Thomas Rogers, 1515, gave to the High Altar of Barnsley 6d., to the roodlight 12d. and to St. Nicholas' light a bushel of barley.

AMPNEY CRUCIS

The church of Ampney Crucis (do not pronounce the p) is of picturesque, indeed quaint appearance because of its steeply pitched chancel roof and low flat nave of not inconsiderable length joining it to the west tower. The reason is of course, that it was built in so many different periods. A unity of a kind, due perhaps to the stone, is achieved outside; but this is not so inside, which is partly plastered, partly scraped, and anyway appears to be somewhat full of unrelated objects, and has a Victorian tiled floor. Even a *corona lucis*, at the west end (I am glad to say) has not been discarded.

The churchyard is well known in that it has the rare and quite well-preserved fifteenth-century cross, complete with gabled head and sculptures which survived the iconoclasts by being hidden and walled up inside the church, and was restored by Canon Howman of Barnsley. For the rest it is rather overshadowed by the buildings of Ampney Park.

There is a Sanctus bellcote, Perpendicular battlements round the nave but no clerestory, and north and south transepts. The north transept has a Decorated window, and lancets on the west; inside there are wall-paintings. The Perpendicular east window has three cinquefoiled lights and straightforward tracery like that at Fairford, and a shaped string-course. The tower has the marks of a formerly high-pitched nave roof, belfry openings, battlements, and gargoyles. The west window of the tower is Perpendicular with deep chamfers. The Saxon doorway cannot be seen outside because of the boiler-house, nor can it be seen to advantage from the inside. There is an Elizabethan tomb with effigies under a canopy, heraldry and strapwork. Before the Dissolution the manor belonged to Tewkesbury Abbey.

The largest of the ring of five bells, inscribed in black letter miniscules: *Protage pura pia Quos convoco virgo maria,* was cast at Bristol in the fifteenth century; another is by Edward Neale, 1660; Thomas Rudhall cast the treble (smallest) in 1780; the others were recast in 1861 and 1908.

AMPNEY ST MARY

A small twelfth-century church with a peculiarly primitive carved tympanum (really a canted lintel) in the north doorway. The church is of considerable character in that it retains a wall painting – faded though it be – to show that labour on Sunday is wounding to Christ; the wounds are visible and the implements of manual labour which inflicted them. A wheelwright is shown truing a spoke held to his eye. This is fourteenth century. Another rare survival is the stone screen with the elbow of one return stall on the south. The church escaped the Perpendicular rebuilding so common in the Cotswolds, and it therefore has more good Decorated remains than is usual, such as the lovely flowing west window. This may be because the church was abandoned by the village after the Black Death, and the church is still isolated on the side of the Ampney Brook, far from habitations.

It was disused from 1879–1913, by which time the restorers were enlightened and sympathetic, and provided an east window by that good artist F. C. Eden.

The bell in the open turret is by Abel Rudhall 1747.

AMPNEY ST PETER

This is the most attractive of the Ampney group of churches for worship, combined with archaeological interest. The nave is late Saxon with a Saxon tower arch, wholly built of through-stones. The light and spacious north aisle was added by Sir Gilbert Scott in 1878 soon after the Rev. T. Daubeney succeeded the Rev. E. A. Daubeney at the close of his 55-year incumbency. The sanctuary has a sumptuous alabaster reredos given in memory of the former, and a floor with a cheerful combination of stone and tile.

There are two bells: one by Edward Neale of Burford, 1677, the other by Thomas Rudhall, 1776. Neale's bell bears the Royal Arms of Charles ii.

HARNHILL

A small church practically in the grounds of the Old Rectory, and approached by a public path between the manor farm and the rectory garden. Its most interesting feature is the carved Norman tympanum, St Michael fighting a dragon. The archangel is winged, and has a sword and shield, and the dragon looks rather a jolly sort with wings, claws, curly tail, and beastly head; perhaps some of the fierceness has rubbed off with age, though it has been quite well protected since the fourteenth century by the porch, which also has the usual niche in its east wall.

Inside, the church looks bigger, and has a rather spacious chancel almost as large as the nave. The Decorated east window has some medieval glass, and there is a Georgian pulpit, 1785.

Two bells, one identified by its shape and mouldings as a fourteenth-century casting; the other by Edward Neale, 1677, with Royal Arms of Charles II.

DRIFFIELD

The church was situated next the mansion of the Hanger family, the enormous garden wall of which runs along the south side of the churchyard. This house was demolished when the then Lord Coleraine sold the material by auction, for purchasers to take down the house, in 1803. The previous Lord Coleraine rebuilt the church, and the eighteenth-century tower remains with its clumsy appearance and over-big modillion cornice, and plain parapet; but the rest of the re-building has not survived. What we have now is a nineteenth-century church by William Butterfield with Lord Coleraine's eighteenth-century furnishings inside.

The south porch has some original fragments. There is a Norman tympanum with diapering and there is a niche in the east wall.

Inside, the box pews and pulpit of 1734 look well in the broad nave. The chancel is more Butterfieldian with polychrome tiles running up the east wall from the floor; but what provides the distinctly holy atmosphere must surely be the complete set of Alexander Gibbs windows favoured by Butterfield in 1865.

In the chancel are many tablets to the Hangers, two of which are intriguing:

> Near this place lieth the body of General
> George Hanger, Lord Coleraine. He lived
> and died a firm Believer in one God
> and in one God only. He was also a
> practical Christian as far as his frail
> nature did allow him to be so. He died
> 31 March 1824 aged 73.

> Here lieth in expectation of the last day
> Gabriel Hanger, Lord Coleraine.
> What manner of man he was
> That day will discover.
> He died 24 January 1773, aged 75.

A ring of three bells; two by Robert Hendley, of Gloucester, second half of the fifteenth century, dedicated to St Mary and St Michael; the tenor is by Abraham Rudhall 1, 1703.

POULTON

At Poulton Priory Farm, a graveyard formerly belonging to the demolished medieval parish church, which was in the middle of the graveyard, is enclosed within buildings now modernized. The farm is on the site of a Gilbertine Priory about which little is known in terms of plan and layout. In 1974 163 gravestones survived, including several table-tombs. The village must have 'moved' and the new church was designed by William Butterfield in the existing centre of population in 1873. In this case he paid strict attention to local stone traditions, and avoided polychrome brickwork which might have been offensive in the Cotswolds.

The organ is by J. W. Walker (1869).

MEYSEY HAMPTON

This is not a typical Cotswold church, indeed it is on the very edge of Cotswold country, but nevertheless a stone place. The church is Early English and Decorated instead of Norman and Perpendicular, unless we count the top of the tower which has battlements and gargoyles.

Cruciform with central tower, nave and chancel of almost equal lengths, and north and south transepts, the church has excellent Decorated work in the chancel. The fine east window has geometrical tracery, and is edged with ballflower. There is a tomb of the same date on the north which may be *c.* 1310. Opposite is work of outstanding quality – a long row of sedilia and the rest, with crocketed canopies. The crossing too, is good, with perfectly matched arches, all of one piece, clear cut and simple. There was a severe restoration by James Brooks in 1872. Most of the windows have clear glass so it does not lack light, though it slightly lacks charm in spite of some entertaining relics like the lectern, Jacobean, with a chain for securing the Bible and the inscription 'Christian Jacketts, 1622', or the provincial monument to Doctor James Vaulx with amusing portrait busts of himself and two wives.

DOWN AMPNEY

This church, which again is not typical of the Cotswolds, is on the Wiltshire edge of the Ampney group and is by far the most delightful building of them all, owing to the interior architecture and furnishings. The setting is flat but very attractive, with splendid trees and water meadows, and the church, approached through a yard full of table tombs and headstones, is very close to the medieval hall-house of the Hungerfords, which was altered by Soane, and beautifully restored after a recent fire.

The west tower is solid-looking in spite of the Early English arcading in the top stage, and it carries a spire. The Perpendicular touch is in the south porch, which is fifteenth century or Tudor, and has angle buttresses with small image niches.

Inside, the church is well lit from a clerestory and the walls are beautifully whitened except the stone work of the arcades, which is decorated with red flowers first painted in the thirteenth century. The capitals of the Transitional arcades have embryonic stiff-leaf ornament above cylindrical piers supporting pointed arches.

The eye is next transfixed by the screens which go right across the entrances to the chancel and transepts. The one on the north is Jacobean, but the rest, however medieval in feeling, actually only date for 1898 onwards and were designed by Charles Ponting, an expert in this field, and brilliantly carved by Harry Hems of Exeter in days when craftsmanship still lived. These were gifts from the Gibbs family who then owned the manor and had by 1907 spent a large sum of money on the church. In the transepts are monuments with effigies, Hungerfords in the north and earlier ones in the south.

The church is hallowed by its association with Ralph Vaughan Williams, and with the Royal Air Force who, in 1974, placed a small window in the north wall in memory of the men who took part in operations from Down Ampney in 1944–45.

Three of the five bells cast by Abraham Rudhall I in 1709 remain; one was recast by Thomas Mears in 1843, the other by Thomas Blackburn in 1899. The oak bellframe is by John Jacques, 1843.

THE UPPER THAMES OR ISIS

Coates, Rodmarton, Kemble, Somerford Keynes, Shorncote,
Kempsford

COATES

The excellent Perpendicular tower looks typically Cotswold and fifteenth century. I find it difficult therefore, to accept an earlier date in spite of the fact that Bigland states it is fourteenth century. The reason for the earlier dating appears to be the inscription on the west face which is said to read: 'Pray for the souls of John Wyatt, formerly rector of Coates, and of Richard his brother, rector of Rodmarton, and for the souls of their parents.' No date for the Wyatts is given or known, but it has been assumed they were fourteenth century,[1] and Atkyns tells us of another inscription that stated that Wyatt built the chancel. The appearance of the chancel with its Decorated windows fits in quite well with a fourteenth-century Wyatt; but the tower certainly does not. It is faced in ashlar and has battlements and very elegant pinnacles with weather vanes. The top stage has openings with ogee shaped hood-moulds with crocketed pinnacles in low relief. The buttresses are diagonal and there are string-courses. On the west are image niches on the buttresses as well as centrally in the middle stage. There are gargoyles and an anthropophagus eating someone up to his middle. The west window is Perpendicular with a four-centred arched head, the west doorway Tudor with a rose in each spandrel which brings it into the late fifteenth or early sixteenth century. Furthermore, on the inside there is a Tudor doorway into the stair turret, besides a splendidly tall tower arch with typical fifteenth-century mouldings, and a stone quadripartite vault. The west window lights the church very well.

The south doorway is Norman, and the arcade dividing the broad south aisle from the nave is Transitional, with round piers and moulded round capitals with pointed arches. The floors are paved with stone flags so the general effect is agreeable. Curtained off on the north side is an abrupt addition, perhaps the chantry chapel of the once powerful Nottingham family, though there is little to show for it except a piscina and a fourteenth-century tomb recess.

References

1 Transactions Bristol & Gloucestershire Archaeological Society, 1926. Vol. XLVIII p. 301.

RODMARTON

The church and churchyard with its table tombs, are set back beyond and to the north of a small green in this unspoiled craftsman's village. The tower, which has a spire, is on the south side, and as we approach we notice that the south side of the nave has an embattled Perpendicular window with grid tracery. On the north side the parapet has gone but some gargoyles remain, and the walls are partly rendered. We enter through the south porch which has an image niche in the north-east corner, and a stoup below.

The interior of the nave is, alas, scraped. There are standard candlesticks in the pews. The chancel is separated by a low Tractarian screen and has a tiled floor, unlike the nave, which is stone flagged. In the north aisle there is a charming monument to Charles George who died in 1807, by Wood of Gloucester, showing the widow looking like a Jane Austen character holding a child by the hand.

KEMBLE

A place best known for its railway station, in fact it is almost the only railway station left in the Cotswolds. The church is mostly notable for its thirteenth-century-style spire which is a hazard to the RAF, and has a beacon light at night. The west doorway under the tower is thirteenth century and on the south there is a large porch protecting a restored south doorway which still has chevrons. The south aisle or chapel, said to have been removed from Ewen, is Perpendicular with four-centred arched windows and a high plinth with roll mouldings and small buttresses. The east window is Perpendicular of the Gloucester type. The north side of the church looks completely nineteenth century, and the interior is a bit of a mix-up. The little eighteenth-century organ-case is a fairly new addition.

Of the ring of six bells, two are modern; one is a late fifteenth-century bell from the Bristol foundry, one by Edward Neale, 1674, one by John Rudhall, 1790 and one by Messrs. Warner, 1869.

Chamber organ, by John England and Hugh Russell, 1785, was repaired by John Coulson, 1966.

SOMERFORD KEYNES

In 685 King Ethelred confirmed a grant of land at Somerford to Aldhelm, Abbot of Malmesbury. The early monasteries were mission stations, and we may assume that Malmesbury had a preaching centre at Somerford and later a stone church was built of which part of the north wall with a primitive doorway still remains. Of this Professor F. M. Stenton says: 'The modern church incorporates a megalithic doorway surmounted by an arch cut out of a single stone and ornamented by narrow parallel mouldings. As Aldhelm is known to have been a builder of churches there is at least a presumption that this doorway represents a church built for the peasantry on his new estate.'[1] The Victoria County History and Dr H. M. Taylor support this view. It is therefore by far the oldest surviving church in the Cotswold area; but, of course, nobody would suppose any such thing on first sight.

The church is set in parkland, with a very old manor house to the immediate west, and a large early nineteenth-century vicarage beyond the ha-ha of the park. It looks medieval; but really the tower was built in the eighteenth century, and the church was restored in 1875–76 by Waller of Gloucester. William the Conqueror granted Somerford to the Bishop of Lisieux who was his personal physician. The Bishop's great niece and heiress married Ralph de Keynes and thus Somerford acquired the name, really Cahaignes from Normandy. In the fourteenth century the manor belonged to the Despensers and then to the Crown, eventually being given to Henry VIII's fifth Queen, the short-lived Katherine Howard. These events made little difference to the villagers, who may have been quietly prosperous towards the end of the Middle Ages. There was at any rate money to spend on the parish church; a porch with the great oak door that still hangs there; and the chancel screen, which today is not a perfect fit, and may be the parclose screen from the north chapel – it was found by Waller under the west gallery, which he removed. This screen has quatrefoil piercings in its bottom section, like the screens at Cirencester. There was also a wooden tower and belfry; but this was taken down when the west tower was built in 1710–13. The fine Perpendicular window may have been in the west wall of the nave and re-erected under the tower when this wall was cut into for the tower arch.

About 1500 the Saxon north door was walled up and plastered over internally, and a great St Christopher painted there, to be reopened on 22 April 1968. John Tame of Fairford left money to Somerford Church, which may have helped to pay for some of this.

Buckler's drawing of 1816 shows a round-headed classical window at the east end of the chancel, and Sir Stephen Glynn in 1870 noted, a three-light east window 'with curious tracery', and a three-light window in the tower, which would be our present Perpendicular one. The east window – now three lancets – must have been altered again by Waller. In 1968 an aumbry was found in the north chapel and a squint south of the chancel arch, suggesting that there was a nave altar where the pulpit now stands.

The dissolution of the monasteries made little difference to Somerford Keynes as Malmesbury Abbey had already parted with their land in the parish. The King sold the rectory, which eventually was bought by Robert Strange of Cirencester in 1570. He was a wealthy wool merchant with a great house in Cirencester and had been appointed High Bailiff of Cirencester by the last Abbot. He bought the manor of Somerford Keynes from Queen Mary in 1554. On 14 June 1654, just a hundred years later, his great grandson, another Robert Strange, died in London of the smallpox. The body of the young squire – he was only 23 – was brought to Somerford for burial in the north aisle. His three sisters erected in his memory the great black and white marble monument with the reclining figure of a young man with his own long hair, and dressed in Cavalier fashion. His uncle Hungerford wrote a long Latin epitaph with the Greek tag, 'Whom the gods love dies young'.[2]

A ring of three bells recently converted into a static chime; two are late medieval castings from the Bristol foundry, the other is by Abel Rudhall, 1747. Also a small sanctus bell by T. Gefferies, early sixteenth century.

References

1 *Oxford History of England*, Vol. I.
2 Geoffrey Gibbon, *The Story of Somerford Keynes and Shorncote*, 1969.

SHORNCOTE

On the Wiltshire edge of the Cotswolds near Cirencester, Shorncote is a very rural hamlet, with sheep grazing up against the churchyard walls, which are indeed Cotswold dry stone walls, though beyond is the flat gravelly plain of Upper Thames. The little church is spiritually and historically rewarding to a quite marked degree considering its size. People ask why tiny places like Shorncote, with a population of about 22 ever since the Black Death, should have been independent parishes with their own church and rector. The answer is that they were ancient manors, and in the Middle Ages every man of position liked to have his own church and appoint his own parson. Built in the reign of Henry 11, with the style moving from Norman to Early English, the church was altered in the fourteenth century, when the west front was rebuilt with its base overlapping the base of the Norman south wall, which was out of perpendicular even at that time.

The entire roof is said to be of this date, *c.* 1370, and also the south porch and the north chapel,¹ all probably the work of the Berkeleys of Beverston who were patrons of the church and held it from the earls of Gloucester. The Berkeley arms occur in the east window. Their chapel has a piscina and credence shelf, and a Decorated window on the north with an elaborately cusped rerearch.

The most interesting exterior feature is the fourteenth-century double bellcote, worked in stone, as is usual on the stone belt, where elsewhere it might have been made of timber. The late Norman chancel arch below retains a screen, presumably the doorway of the original rood-screen. Inside the chancel are remains of twelfth-century wall paintings simulating masonry with flower devices, a rare Easter Sepulchre set in the splay of a Norman window, and floor tiles by William Butterfield, alas! hidden by an ugly blue carpet. Butterfield restored the church in 1882–83, giving his services free of charge,² and designing the pews more comfortably for kneeling than sitting. There is a seventeenth-century pulpit mended in 1727, a Charles 11 walnut carved high-back chair, and a Hanoverian Royal Arms in plaster.

One bell in open turret by one of the Rudhalls (not examined at close quarters).

References

1 C. E. Ponting (Wiltshire Archaeological Magazine Vol. XII).
2 Geoffrey Gibbon, *The Story of Somerford Keynes and Shorncote*, 1969.

KEMPSFORD

The church consists of a Norman ashlar nave retaining four original deeply splayed windows, north and south doorways, flat pilaster buttresses at the west end and a string-course with zigzag running over the pilasters. There was a Norman castle just south-west of the church. The manor was given by Henry Duke of Lancaster to the Collegiate Church at Leicester. The chancel has a three-light window with a sexfoil in a circle, a form of *c.* 1300 and very distinctive, also a Decorated window with reticulated tracery on the north containing medieval glass of the Virgin being taught to read by St Anne, and single lancets with cinquefoiled and cusped rere-arches. The chapel was opened on the south in 1858 by G. E. Street, who also designed the attractive choir stalls.

The wonder of the church, however, is the Perpendicular tower, wrongly attributed to the time of John of Gaunt and in reality belonging to the great period of Perpendicular building in the Cotswolds in the mid-late fifteenth century. A more probable tradition says that it was built by a mason from Oxford (see Introduction; Perpendicular, p. 43). Resemblances to other Perpendicular churches can be seen; but here all the effort seems to have gone into the tower. Its central position is similar to Fairford and Cricklade, its nearest neighbours; but its vault is more elaborate than Fairford with ornamental bosses and extra ribs. It is only relevent to compare the lower part of the tower at Cricklade (as the upper part is much later) and that resembles Fairford, as indeed do other features of the church; in this connection Kempsford is the odd one out.

Kempsford has an open parapet and diagonal pinnacles and buttresses. The big north and south Perpendicular windows have tiers of tracery in two transoms, two sub-arches intersected by mullions as at the west end of Gloucester Cathedral, and the point of the main arch is divided in the centre by a mullion as in the porch at Cirencester. The window mouldings generally, however, are not so refined and elaborate as they are at Fairford, and the windows do not have four-centred arched heads which is typical of the maturest Cotswold Perpendicular style. The clerestory windows have straight heads; the tower windows are pointed, a single light rectangular window resembles Stanton Harcourt. The Perpendicular north porch has a niche with ogee arch and pinnacles; but it looks as if it may be a moved Easter Sepulchre, and is a clumsy affair when compared with the work of this period.

THE FROME VALLEY

Cranham, Brimpsfield, Elkstone, Syde, Miserden, Winstone,
Edgeworth, Sapperton, Frampton Mansell, Chalford, Stroud,
Uplands, Randwick, King's Stanley, Leonard Stanley, Selsley

This is the most spectacular of all the river valleys in the Cotswolds, with its excessively steep banks and hanging beech woods. It created Stroud as an international centre of the cloth trade; but its source lies far away on the high escarpment at Cranham. It flows back almost to Cirencester before turning west and heading for the Severn.

CRANHAM

The church is at the end of a rather bleak common away from the village, which is situated on steep hills near well-kept beech woods. It has a certain charm, though altered in 1894–95, when a north aisle was added to match the Perpendicular south aisle. The strong little tower has Perpendicular belfry openings, and a four-centred restored Perpendicular west window with deeply hollow mouldings and a dripmould with carved flower stops. The most intriguing things on the west face of the tower are two pairs of sheep shears carved in the stone, indicating, I suppose, that it may have been a wool merchant's gift which enabled the tower to be built in the fifteenth century.

There is a fine provincial and lively baroque monument to Obadiah Done, 1738, inside the church, with cherubs holding wooden trumpets and palm leaves gilded with gold leaf. Another tablet is to Thomas Dyer-Edwards, who restored the church, turned Catholic, and left Prinknash Abbey to the Benedictines from Caldey Island in 1928.

BRIMPSFIELD

Brimpsfield is very high up but in an attractive setting. We have to walk across a field to get to the church, with the wooded site of the castle on our right. The manor was given by William I to Walter Giffard, whose family held it till one rebelled against Edward II, and his castle was demolished. The site has remained untouched for a very long time, and we are more conscious of these long-dead Giffards than of anything more recent as we approach the church and find inside, as we expected, further evidence of this warlike but pious family. Three medieval tombstones were removed from the churchyard in 1970. The large stone, bearing a long sword carved in relief, must surely commemorate one of the Giffard lords in the twelfth or thirteenth century. It now rests in the chancel just beyond the squint from the chapel where the huge stone *mensa* has been replaced, and at which the Giffard lords and ladies could well have received the Sacrament. The other two tombstones bear ring-crosses of Maltese shape; the smaller was probably a headstone, and the larger, with an elongated shaft to the cross, a flat grave slab. Their dates cannot be fixed exactly; but they are of the fourteenth century or earlier. Characterized by this special form of cross, they were probably from a workshop of a local school of craftsmen.

There is a central tower which is fifteenth century, supported partly on Norman work. This gives the church a very unusual appearance. There is no east window, a peculiarity shared by near-by Winstone. The Perpendicular font has buttresses comparable with Syde. The walls are lime-washed. The Tractarian choir-screen, however, seems now incongruous.

Four bells, one from the medieval foundry at Exeter, a great rarity in these parts, probably fifteenth century; another by Thomas Gefferies, Bristol, early sixteenth century; and two dating from the present century.

ELKSTONE

This church has for long been the best known of the Cotswold churches for its Norman work, and rightly so because the Norman plan is undisturbed except for the addition of a Perpendicular western tower and a porch on the south. It also retains a stone vault over the chancel, and there was a central tower, albeit all rather small-scale. Its plan can therefore be compared with Hampnett, Coln St Dennis, and Hazleton.

It dates from *c.* 1160, the time of the Cotswold Romanesque renaissance, if it can be so called. There is an exuberance of spirit in the carving of the primitive grotesque heads all over the building. The billeted corbel table shows the original height of the eaves and is carved with grotesques which are similar to the heads carved round the arch of the south doorway. This doorway is very close to the one at Siddington. Can it be that there was a particular mason who perhaps learnt his craft at Cirencester Abbey, which was building at this moment, and then worked here and at Siddington, even ending up in the nave at Malmesbury Abbey where the hood-moulds over the arches of the arcades (*c.* 1170) have billets and beast-head stops, and are surmounted by grotesque heads at the apexes very like the ones over the top of the arches of the doors at Elkstone and Siddington? This Elkstone grotesque has fangs, in fact all of them here seem inclined to be fanged. The arch of the door has an inner roll moulding, and the snouts of the creatures lap over the roll. Two of them are perfectly human, male and female; but the rest are inventive to a degree. They are excessively like the ones at Siddington; but the latter do not look quite so good, perhaps owing to part restoration, and the tympana in both cases lack the sophistication of the carving of the beakheads. The Elkstone tympanum has Christ in Majesty with all four Evangelists' emblems plus the Agnus Dei and the hand of God the Father. The stone is really a lintel with a canted top and round the edge is a trailing leaf pattern, rather like work on the South Cerney doorway which in its turn is closer to the more accomplished carvings at Malmesbury.

In the chancel the vault is crowned centrally by a boss with four grotesque fanged heads looking down the ribs, and tied with a beaded buckle to make it look more secure to people who had never stood under a stone vault before; what a delightful invention! The chancel arch has beast-head stops to the hood-mould, and an order of two-dimentional chevrons as at Bishop's Cleeve, and also like Bishop's Cleeve, there is an embattled motif. Here it is round the east window on the outside. The inside of this exquisite little window has 'paterae' or marguerites on the outer edge of a roll moulding so they fold back. The Rev. F. W. Potto Hicks, a former rector and archaeologist, said he had only seen such motifs at the old church at Churchdown, and this I can corroborate though they have been interfered with at Churchdown, in that they are not all *in situ.*

The porch is an addition of the fourteenth century, as is the vault in the 'choir' because the Norman tower collapsed. Over the vaults is a columbarium. During the fifteenth century four Perpendicular windows replaced the original small lights, that on the south-east of the nave lighted an altar, the remains of which were removed soon after 1850. The greatest Perpendicular alteration however, was of course the addition of the splendid fifteenth-century west tower, with its angle-buttresses graded to the middle of the bell-stage whence they ascend as pilasters. Though some 300 hundred years later than the Norman work, the medieval mind still enjoyed grotesque humour, as can be seen in the gargoyles of the battlemented parapet and the quaint figures on two of the set-offs, one with a citole and the other with a recorder, each with a grotesque animal on either side. The west window has a pronounced hollow moulding. A mutilated image of the Virgin rests on the outer sill. The hood of the window springs from winged angels bearing the arms of Acton and Poyntz, families which held the advowson.[1] The Perpendicular tower arch has piers with many concave and ovolo mouldings, most complex in plan with at least a dozen different planes. The little cap of the interior shaft of the window has mouldings as concave as those at Northleach. The fifteenth-century font is of a pattern common in the neighbourhood; but its craftsmanship and condition are exceptionally good.

In the churchyard there are two excellent seventeenth-century table tombs of the Poole family near the south-east angle of the tower.

The priests' house exists (fourteenth century, with an upper hall roof, altered in Tudor times).

A medieval oak bellframe for four bells installed when the tower was built, has been preserved: it received additions in the seventeenth and twentieth centuries. Parts of medieval bellframes remain in many Cotswold Churches although the bells they contain have been recast subsequently. At Elkstone two of the five bells are by Edward Neale, 1657, who seems to have been unusually busy during the Commonwealth regime; the others are modern.

References

1 F. W. Potto Hicks, Guide to Elkstone Church.

SYDE

This ancient little church set on the steep bank opposite Caudle Green, has a saddleback tower, with an outside stair. It is only separated from the manor by a tithe barn cum-priest's house.

The unspoiled nave has lime-washed walls, eighteenth-century box pews, and a Royal Arms, which all provide an intimate atmosphere. The Perpendicular font is a winner; it has a regular plinth not unlike the base of a tower in miniature, and buttresses. There is a fifteenth-century closing ring in the north door, and a fifteenth-century glass roundel of Santiago de Compostela. The tiny chancel was rebuilt, and is now dominated by a new stained-glass window of the Virgin.

Two fourteenth-century bells by unidentified founders, one inscribed with the alphabet, the other: *Protege Virgo Maria quos convoco Sca Maria*; these two bells hang in a medieval oak frame; above them is a bell by Thomas Rudhall, 1771.

MISERDEN

A very early church with Saxon remains, though most of its archaeological interest was destroyed in the drastic nineteenth-century restoration. The west tower is Perpendicular and has diagonal buttresses on the west, and bell openings of the kind that are divided centrally by the vertical mullion. In spite of the lime-washed walls and stone floors the interior is very dark, owing to the poor Victorian stained-glass windows. The sanctuary is beautiful, with an English Altar and riddel posts by F. E. Howard; but by far the most interesting things about the church are its monuments.

In the south chancel chapel is the very fine tomb-chest of Sir William Sandys, who died in 1640. His and his wife's effigies are exquisitely carved in Derbyshire alabaster, possibly by Edward Marshall. Children are carved round the sides. There is also the effigy of William Kingston who died in 1614; painted stone, and carved by the local sculptor Baldwin of Stroud, with his feet on a delightful goat which eats a cabbage. The accoutrements above have been removed, it is hoped, for safety, but a hatchment remains up against the roof ridge.

Outside the church is the 1914 War Memorial by Sir Edwin Lutyens; a tall Cross.

WINSTONE

A small church in high, rather bleak Cotswold country, redeemed by a cedar tree close at hand on the south, and nice headstones in the churchyard. The interior is not pleasing as it suffered a most cruel restoration and was scraped by the Wallers in 1876. It is, however, Anglo-Saxon cum Norman, and the monolithic north jamb of the chancel arch has to be seen to be believed. There is no east window. Everything is simple and strong, with indications of Saxon work.

Three bells; tenor from the Worcester foundry, *c.* 1410 with 'Royal Heads' stops (cf. Coberley) inscribed *Katerine Prece nos servet Cristus a nece*; treble by John of Gloucester, *c.* 1350, inscribed: *Eternis Annis resonet campana Iohannis;* second by Thomas Rudhall, 1771.

The late eighteenth-century organ was made in Germany.

EDGEWORTH

Yet another church in this area with Saxon remains; a few through-stones in the north blocked doorway which are not exactly spectacular. However, there is quite a splendid Perpendicular west tower, and a Norman chancel with corbel table of grotesque heads, both features characteristic of the Cotswolds. The tower has battlements and gargoyles. We also notice with pleasure the agreeable effect of the flat flagstones round the church in the area of the south porch, forming paving, and the incised gravestones, one very shelly, carved with a cross and chalice for a priest in the fourteenth century, and another flat gravestone with a copper plate beautifully lettered by Hamlett of Stroud for Sarah Cripps, who died in 1828.

We go in through the south door, which has Norman chevrons at right angles. The interior, I regret to say once more, has been disastrously scraped, and is very dark; but it is well cared-for, and there is a modern screen, and the original medieval poppy-head bench ends have been copied throughout. The Victorian candle brackets are also attractive. The chancel has been re-modelled with elaborate rere-arches to the windows, and a stone communion rail. Some medieval glass in a window on the north.

A complete ring of five bells by Abraham Rudhall 1, 1716. cf. Colesbourne.

SAPPERTON

The church stands in a romantic situation on a terrace at the edge of the thickly wooded Frome valley. The view down the valley towards Stroud is unsurpassed, and was shared before its demolition in 1730 by the great manor house of the Atkyns family. The first Lord Bathurst bought the manor in that year, and it is still part of the estate on the edge of Cirencester Park. Before this happened, however, the Atkyns family had largely rebuilt the church in the early part of Queen Anne's reign. From the outside, with its many round-headed windows, it looks substantially of this date, although it is older in origin, and has a central tower with a spire.

As we approach from higher up and walk down the churchyard path, we must pass between the graves of the craftsmen Ernest Gimson, who died in 1919, on our left, and his friends the Barnsley brothers, on our right. Their work has achieved an international reputation and was inspired by local traditions and their admiration for William Morris.

When we enter the church we realize at once that the interior is going to be even more rewarding than the exterior, for it is beautifully furnished with woodwork taken from the manor house. Except for the linen-fold benches near the font, all the pews have bench-ends with Jacobean caryatids – though the majority are male – and other Renaissance motifs. The high wall opposite Sir Robert Atkyn's monument is panelled, and so is the family pew in its gallery. There is a frieze with strapwork panels and small shields of arms of the Whittington family, below the wagon roof, which is lit by wrought-iron rings bearing hanging electric light bulbs. The floor of the chancel is stone, and it is hoped that a stone floor can be inserted in the north transept. The whole atmosphere is very pleasing, and ashlar walls are flooded with light from the clear glass in the classical windows.

There are three splendid monuments. Sir Robert Atkyns, the County historian, who died in 1711, lies in effigy on his elbow, his hand resting on a book, which looks smaller than his *Ancient and Present State of Gloucestershire*. The other monuments are in the north transept to the Poole family. Sir Henry Poole, who died in 1616, has a great canopied Renaissance tomb with many effigies.

A ring of three bells; treble dedicated to St John, by an early four-teenth-century Gloucester founder; second dedicated to St Margareta (*sic*) by John Barber of Salisbury, or one of his successors early fifteenth century; tenor by Abraham Rudhall 1, 1698.

FRAMPTON MANSELL

On the edge of the Frome valley before it becomes the early indus-trialized Golden Valley, just above the railway line, and the great lake at the bottom with its swans, stands a church built in 1843 by the Lord Bathurst of the day in the Romanesque style then fashionable. We can approach from above down a steep lavender-edged path, and look right through the open-work of the top of the *campanile*. The interior is broad and suitable for preaching, with a stone floor and small apsidal sanctuary.

CHALFORD

The church is beside the river Frome and its canals in the Golden Valley, close to old mills and a round house; on the opposite bank are hanging beech woods.

The small broach spire, covered in tiles and sprocketed, looks foreign. To one side is an eighteenth-century church room, which is also the date of the north arcade with its tall classical Roman Doric columns of six bays with tunnel vaults gabled transversely. This is surprising, as is the rest of the interior, which is Arts-and-Crafts and reminds us that Peter Waals had his workshop in Chalford. The font is by William Simmonds, with cover by Norman Jewson and silver-work by George Hart; the lectern inlaid with ivory and mother-of-pearl by Peter Waals; the stained glass by Edward Payne.

The only cast steel bells in the Cotswolds, a ring of six by Naylor, Vickers and Company, 1857.

STROUD

St Lawrence's Church, Stroud, is a town church which could be anywhere. Except for the fourteenth-century west tower and spire, it is rather ugly outside, a bit rock-faced with Bath stone dressings and Broseley tiles. The interior is much more impressive, like a basilica, with columns of blue Pennant stone and Byzantine-style capitals, carved by the local nineteenth-century carver Joshua Wall. The real *tour de force* is the screen of 1912, which spreads, grandly canopied, across the whole building, below an enormous Rood. The east window is by Clayton & Bell; below it is a gilded reredos by George Gilbert Scott, the younger, very splendid.

In the south transept there is a monument by Samuel Baldwin of Stroud, to a Jacobean gentleman whose painted and gilded effigy kneels with wide-open staring eyes.

One of the windows should be noted; it is the one in the extreme north-west corner of the north aisle with glass by that talented and tragic young man, J. C. N. Bewsey, commemorating the Stantons in 1913, with glowing colours, St Martin and St George. And surely the font-cover must be an Ernest Gimson-Peter Waals design?

On the north there is a seemingly very private and very beautiful little churchyard with monolithic table-tombs, trees and a view, probably about to be spoiled by the erection of a new vicarage.

UPLANDS

Uplands Church is situated on the steep bank where the Slad Valley enters Stroud. It was designed by Temple Moore in 1908, and his Royal Academy drawing (preserved in the church) of the east aspect looks very delightful. Indeed it is a delightful building, coming some years after he had designed a house formerly called Gwynfa, for the Vicar of near-by Painswick.

The stone interior is light, spacious and beautiful, with a stone floor, only chairs to sit on, and absolutely no stained glass windows at all. The nave is broad, with a north aisle under the same sloping roof, and on the south transverse gables, on the east a projecting chancel and on the west a tower and broach-spire. It shows some of his idiosyncrasies, like a pretence miniature triforium tunnel giving interest to the outer walls.

RANDWICK

Randwick church is on a steep hill among other equally precipitous hills, mostly quite densely populated suburbs of Stroud.

The churchyard is a small 'conservation area' for wild flowers, and there are table-tombs. The tower is rather ordinary Perpendicular with diagonal buttresses and battlements; but the rest is mostly nineteenth century, and a very broad south aisle was added in *c.* 1894 for there is an almost unbelievable inscription which states that the foundation stone was laid 'in memory of the Rev. John Elliott, 72 years Vicar of this parish, on 24 May 1893'.

Inside the church there is a curiously happy atmosphere, and every wall is festooned with objects, some very pleasing like the Queen Anne Royal Arms, others more ephemeral.

KING'S STANLEY

Really, King's Stanley is just in the vale; but it is closely allied to Selsley and Leonard Stanley, and I prefer to include the group in the Cotswolds, although their affinities are nearer to cloth than wool.

The churchyard has clipped yew trees and some table tombs; but the church looks a bit dull from the outside, in spite of a seventeenth-century date on one of the buttresses. However, the inside is rewarding, and it has every sign that G. F. Bodley was responsible for the restoration in 1876. The wagon roof of the nave, and the roof of the south aisle have Bodley's painted decorations, and the organ case was designed by Bodley, and very good it is, made by a local carpenter called Liddiatt.

LEONARD STANLEY

Roger Berkeley chose this site just below the escarpment to found an Augustinian priory in the 1120s. The small chapel now used as a farm building to the south-west was the original parish church. It is quite clear the present church was a monastic one, and inside the nave it can be seen how far west the original screen stood, leaving only a portion of the nave for lay worshippers.

It is of very great interest because of its Norman remains, including two sculptured capitals, and a third one in the porch. It has a wide aisleless nave, and crossing with a massive central tower, transepts and chancel. The north doorway has two chevroned orders and a hood-mould with beast-head stops. The chancel is of two bays with Norman vaulting shafts with carved capitals, dating from the second quarter of the twelfth century, one of the Nativity showing the Virgin in bed and the other of the woman wiping Christ's feet, His hand raised in blessing. This figure has been compared by Professor Zarnecki with the wooden head of Christ at South Cerney, perhaps brought back by a pilgrim to Compostela. There is nothing else like it in the Cotswolds, though there may be in Herefordshire. A third capital, evidently by the same hand, is preserved in the north porch, high up. It seems to represent prophets sitting in an arcade with corbels and holding a scroll.

The general aspect of the church inside is light and gracious, with lime-washed walls. The sanctuary was restored by Bodley and has his favoured floor of black and white marble.

SELSLEY

The third church in the Stanley group is entirely the work of G. F. Bodley. It is sited up on the hill next Stanley Park and overlooking the Marlings' former mill (also designed by Bodley) at Ebley. From the vale, Selsley Church stands up very well half-way up the escarpment, and the converse view from the lychgate above it is equally spectacular, looking down so that the 'French' saddleback tower is clear against the sky, for this was built during Bodley's early French period.

Bodley had made friends with the Pre-Raphaelite brotherhood in 1858, and here he gave William Morris his first commission for making ecclesiastical stained glass. Philip Webb provided the scheme for the whole church, with detailed design for the marvellous Creation window at the west end. Webb was particularly good at drawing animals. Besides these two, the other artists were Burne-Jones, Rossetti, Ford Madox Brown and Campfield.

Bodley designed the pews and choir-stalls, which have poppy-head and fleur-de-lys finials, and delightful Gothic elbow rests like miniature bartizans, also the communion rails, door iron-work, Forest-stone font, and inlaid marble pulpit; but the parclose screen to the north chapel and the west inner porch are later and rather unfortunate additions. The church was built in 1861-62, with local labour, the contractors were Harrison of King's Stanley, with stone carving by Joshua Wall. The woodwork was done by William English, and the ironwork by T. J. Chew, both of Stroud.

THE AVEN VALLEY

Cherington, Avening, Horsley, Woodchester, Minchinhampton, Rodborough

Like the Frome or Golden Valley, the Aven (or Little Avon) valley is industrial, in that it has long been associated with the cloth trade. Horsley church is described rather than Nailsworth because it is more interesting architecturally.

CHERINGTON

The Early English chancel is a delight in itself, almost like a separate building with its higher pitched roof. Not perhaps so grand as some East Anglian chancels of this date, *c.* 1230–50; but in its way perfect, with lancet windows linked inside and out with moulded stone string-courses and hood-moulds, and so grouped in the east wall as to indicate the future development of a more complicated window. It is unfortunate that the interior walls of the chancel are now scraped of plaster, which does not provide a very satisfactory background for the windows, nor indeed for the provincial baroque monuments. However, the nave is plastered, and here there is a lower pitched roof in the Perpendicular style of the fifteenth century, very splendidly carved, and supported on carved stone corbel heads. The churchyard is pretty and grows primroses in the Spring.

One of the four bells was recast in 1870; the tenor is by Abel Rudhall, 1744; the others by Edward Neale, 1672 and 1683, on one of them is the Royal Arms of Charles II.

AVENING

On leaving Cherington, which is an upland village, the road to Avening immediately begins to descend into that border land between Cotswold and Severn vale, full of deep ravines and wooded banks. Avening had a mill below the big house, but the mill pond is overgrown, and signs of past industry have disappeared. The church, however, shows many signs of present prosperity.

It stands on a bank, and the upward slope of the churchyard is green grass where the tombstones have been cleared for mowing, and reassembled to the west higgledy-piggledy. This is one solution to the problem, and anyway better than assembling them in a row leaning against a boundary wall. A new part of the churchyard has been opened on the east, and has a pretty approach.

Soon after the Norman conquest Avening was given by the

Conqueror's wife Matilda to the nuns of La Trinité, or the Abbaye aux Dames, founded by her at Caen in Normandy. The church which was then built consisted of a chancel, central tower and nave. This plan survives in several instances on the Cotswolds; but Avening is one of the most complete, for not only does it have a stone rib-vaulted crossing, it also has a vaulted chancel. Hampnett and Elkstone have vaulted chancels, and at Coln St Dennis there is a pier in each corner which once must have supported a vault. Other examples of the remains of Norman towers are at Great Rissington, Leonard Stanley, South Cerney, Withington, and Stowell. In addition at Avening, which is perhaps about 1080, there is a small north aisle, originally a chapel, with an arcade of two round arches supported on a fairly massive round column, but low, with a scalloped cushion cap. On the south side against the east wall of the nave there must have been a nave altar and the remains of the Norman arch behind survive with rich mouldings like the north doorway; this is once again used for the purpose for which it was intended. The transepts were added in the thirteenth century. The chancel was lengthened in the fourteenth century and the vault continued with carved bosses. The east window is in early Decorated style; but it certainly did not exist before the 1888 restoration because there is a photograph preserved in the museum in the south transept, showing an east window without tracery, besides an enormous gallery over the north side of the nave, box-pews below, and a terrible arrangement of heating stoves with almost horizontally inclined pipes suspended through the air in the central space. The 1902 restoration by Micklethwaite was sympathetic. The floor of the nave is now open with chairs and elegant parquet, no doubt provided by the late Lord Lee of Fareham, along with his banner of the Order of the Bath. In the museum transept there are some vigorous baroque tablets to the Driver family by Reeve of Gloucester, seventeenth century. In the north transept is Samuel Baldwin's effigy of the erstwhile pirate and highwayman Henry Brydges, who is said to have found it convenient to keep his horses shod 'hind-before'.

A ring of six bells; two from the Bristol foundry, 1628; two by Abel Rudhall, 1756; two by Mears and Stainbank, 1903.

HORSLEY

On the edge of the Cotswolds above the cloth-milling town of Nailsworth, the church stands next the site of a Norman priory; but the

only part of the existing building earlier than the Dissolution is the
rather solid-looking Perpendicular west tower, which has diagonal
buttresses, and four string-courses continuing round the buttresses
in the approved Cotswold manner, and battlements and pinnacles.

The remainder of the church, built in 1838–39, is the work of
Thomas Rickman, the Early Victorian Quaker architect, who
established the still-used terms of Early English, Decorated and
Perpendicular, since nobody has thought of any better way of classi-
fying medieval church architecture. It is broad and looks as if it was
built as a preaching church in rather thin Gothic clothes. The
Tractarian screen and choir are of course, later alterations. Under the
tower are a couple of good baroque tablets of an eighteenth-century
clothier family called Davis.

WOODCHESTER

One of the nineteenth-century rectors thought St Paul had preached
in Woodchester.[1] He reasoned that we are told St Paul went on many
voyages and therefore he must have come to the Roman Governor's
house in Britain. Anyway it is quite reasonable to suppose there has
been a Christian church on the site of the old church since Christian-
ity came to England. It would be interesting to excavate on the site
to see what Saxon remains there are. There is documentary evidence
for a priest in the ninth century, and he is named, and must therefore be one of the first-known vicars in England. What remains of
the old church is unused. Hardly anyone protested at its demolition
in 1860, except an architect, who wrote to the newspaper to complain
of the vandalism in destroying this Norman church. Most people in
Woodchester, however, who belonged to the Church of England,
felt their noses put out by the Roman Catholics who had built a new
church and two monasteries in South Woodchester, and wished to
show what the Church of England could do for itself after the Oxford
Movement.

What we have left in the famous churchyard where lies the best
Roman pavement in England, is a Norman chancel arch and north
doorway, and some interesting gravestones; there is a fine symbolic
tomb in the north-east corner with a triangle to represent the Trinity
in a circle for Eternity.

Historically this little church had one or two excitements. In the
sixteenth century it suffered from the Puritans, and it was stated that
in 1594, the 'Woman was taken from the porch'. This must have

been an image of the Virgin Mary. In the Civil War, Col. Massey's soldiers dragged the rector out of the church, and made him walk bare-foot to prison in Gloucester. In 1793, Lysons discovered the Roman pavement, and this received the attention due to it from a civilized age; but seven years later, in 1800, a Woodchester man was hanged in Gloucester for cutting cloth on the racks at Mr Wathen's mill.

There was considerable enthusiasm for the new church building. The architect, S. S. Teulon, had been building Tortworth House for Lord Ducie in 1849. Woodchester Church comes after Teulon's other Cotswold churches, Kingscote (1851), Uley (1857–8), and Newington Bagpath (1858), and is more or less contemporary with Nympsfield and Huntley (1863). The builder was Harrison of King's Stanley, who also built Selsley Church for Bodley the year before, where the stone carving was by Joshua Wall of King's Stanley, and no doubt these capitals are too. The consecration on 24 September 1863 was performed before the building was completed to fit in with the Bishop's plans; even so he missed his train in Gloucester and rode over on horseback. The Chancellor was also late, and his registrar, having missed the Bishop, came on by a second train, delaying matters even more. Four stained-glass windows are original; one shows its Anglican character with a chalice on the altar and a kneeling Virgin in the Communion of Saints. Three in the south wall by Preedy, Lavers and Barraud are excellent. On the north Teulon's special designs for glazing with clear glass are still seen to advantage. The geometrical decorated style of the arcade is dynamic and is transmogrified into the roof which is solidly trussed with oak hammer-beams, typically Teulon. The monuments were removed from the old church; several are by well-known sculptors, Ricketts of Gloucester and Paty of Bath.

References

1 Rev. W. N. R. J. Beck, *A History of Woodchester*, 1972.

MINCHINHAMPTON

On high ground between the Aven and Frome valleys there stands what is in many ways one of the most interesting churches on the Cotswolds; but it is not typical, and does not have good Norman or Perpendicular work. Minchinhampton is situated on the edge of the

Cotswolds where they descend to the cloth-milling valleys, and the church has the look of having belonged in the past, and of still belonging, to a prosperous community.

We are told that the Abbess of Caen ran a great many sheep at Minchinhampton in Norman times. In the twelfth century the church was rebuilt or enlarged, cruciform in plan with a central tower, which now dates from the fourteenth century, and has a curious truncated spire which was taken down to this height in 1563, and crowned with a stone coronet. The transepts are also fourteenth-century; the one on the south is remarkably beautiful. Nearly the whole of its south wall is filled with a splendid Decorated window; the upper part of the tracery retains a wheel-like rose with ogee motifs, but the lower part is restored. The walls either side have continuous windows divided by buttresses outside supporting the stone vault within, really stone transverse arches crossing scissor-wise like a wooden roof. Under the tower the crossing has a tierceron-star vault with carved bosses, and delicate shafts rising from the floor with foliated capitals. The four chamfered arches die off into their responds.

Below the great window in the south transept, which is filled with glass by Hardman, are two most elaborate Decorated tombs with ogee foils and floral cusps, below crocketed ogee arches. The tomb chests have quatrefoils carved in low-relief, and the richness contrasts with the simple clear-cut effigies of the Knight and Lady. He is in bascinet and surcoat with a heater shield, legs crossed and feet on a lion; she wears a wimple. They are perhaps Peter and Matilda de la Mere, early fourteenth-century donors of the transept. The Decorated north transept also has a tomb recess, now blocked by the organ.

The aisled nave was rebuilt in 1842, and now has an elegant and harmonious appearance. The chancel was altered by the great William Burges in the 1860's. He provided a sumptous rere-arch to the east window, with glass by Hardman. The chancel roof is beautifully painted by F. C. Eden, who also designed the screen, and the Altar is by Geoffrey Webb, so the church has been embellished by the best ecclesiastical artists for many years. The windows in the nave are by Herbert Bryans, a pupil of Kempe, except one by Edward Payne.

At the west end of the church is a new Parish Room designed by Peter Falconer and beautifully built by Morgans, Walker & Morgans, in 1974. It is an octagonal stone building with a sprocketed stone roof culminating in a finial, ceiled underneath in cedar-wood. It has direct communication with the west door.

RODBOROUGH

The Perpendicular tower has battlements and diagonal buttresses, and a Tudor west door opposite some good stone houses; otherwise the church was rebuilt in 1842 and restored in 1895. There is a nice Jacobean pulpit, two Stuart chairs, one with the Royal arms, an 'English altar' and riddles, a nice organ case and a Willement window. Here Benjamin Bucknall, the architect translator of Viollet-le-Duc, was baptized in 1833.

TETBURY DISTRICT

Tetbury, Beverston, Westonbirt, Didmarton, Leighterton,
Boxwell, Lasborough, Newington Bagpath, Kingscote

TETBURY

The parish church was rebuilt between 1777 and 1781, which is an unusual date for such an undertaking. The old church was in a bad state and there had been an attempt to restore it; but the architect, James Gibbs, called in as umpire, pronounced that the work was not satisfactory. This gave the go-ahead to the people, including the vicar, who wished to start again from scratch. Francis Hiorn of Warwick was the architect and we have a very early example of quite convincing Gothic Revival.

There are, however, considerable differences between it and later Gothic Revival churches, particularly in plan. The body of the church is surrounded by a passage, more like a theatre or opera house, with doors which open into box-pews. There is no way in to some of these boxes from the central aisle, and they can only be entered by a private door from the passage. This idea is really the same as the private outside staircase – often built in the eighteenth century – to enable the upper classes to enter their own gallery. The other difference is that this large auditorium was built as a preaching church, and there is a great feeling of theatrical space inside. The wooden columns are clustered, with an inner core of iron, and so they do not obstruct the views, although they seem numerous, and the colour is like a faded yellow print. It is unfortunate aesthetically that there has been an attempt – which alas succeeds – to make the church more suitable for Anglican worship, and there is now a screen and choir stalls and organ instead of the pulpit and reading desk in the last bays of the nave, thus destroying the original effect of the shallow apsed sanctuary. However, the decalogue and picture by the American President of the Royal Academy, Benjamin West, are back in their right places, as are the most magnificent brass chandeliers of 1781 – London work – each carrying 36 lights, now rescued and re-hung lower and therefore better than before. All the windows are by Wailes except one Clayton & Bell. There is a fine set of plate from St Saviour's which includes two chalices, two patens, and one flagon, Birmingham 1847 and 1848, by John Hardman, all to Pugin's design, and this gives us the clue to St Saviour's; but before we go on, it must be stated that the marvellous tower and spire of the parish church were rebuilt from the ground in 1890.

St Saviour's is a little, though not so very little, Tractarian church for the poor of 1848. The vicar of Tetbury in the nineteenth century was John Frampton from 1828 to 1881, and his churchmanship was low, and suited the parish church, as it was then. He had, however, Father Charles Lowder as curate, who afterwards went to London Docks and became known and loved by thousands. St Saviour's is the result of the young Father Lowder's high church aspirations, and it remains to this day in a perfectly unspoiled condition with every Tractarian thought materialized intact. Pugin was employed with Hardman to provide the reredos and sanctuary roof; but the rest is a little masterpiece by Samuel Whitfield Daukes, architect of the near-by Cirencester Royal Agricultural College and Chapel. There is a screen; all the pews have poppy heads and each one is different, and the backs are open with quatrefoils and incline the sitter into a kneeling posture. The windows are by O'Connor, with his signature in the brilliant east window and also in the west, and pleasant *grisaille* windows in the aisles, and a baptism behind the font. The chain of the font cover has a weighted dove to balance. There are lots of details which give pleasure; but most important of all the atmosphere is still there, although the church is redundant.

BEVERSTON

Here is a Saxon carving that shows the delicate linear manner and fluttering draperies of the Winchester school of painting. It is the figure of Christ, now built into the south wall of the tower, about five feet high, and shows Christ full length holding a long stemmed cross or Resurrection banner. His robe blows out like fluttering streamers. It dates from the first half of the eleventh century and resembles a figure of Christ (*c.*1025) at Bristol Cathedral.[1] The castle or manor was occupied by Earl Godwin in 1051, though the present castle dates from *c.* 1225, and belonged to the Berkeleys.

The church has a south aisle and porch, restored Perpendicular windows either side, with eye-catching tracery of many cusps. The chancel is Decorated, with ballflower round the outer edge of the south windows, an ogee-headed priests' doorway, and an east window with Decorated tracery resembling the chapel window in the castle. The tower has Perpendicular battlements, pinnacles, and belfry windows of deep chamfers, divided perpendicularly in the middle of their arches. On the north side the north window of the transept or Berkeley chapel, is square headed with a stopped label, and three lights with cinquefoil heads. Near-by are some thirteenth-century coffin lids, with incised crosses, built into the masonry walls.

The great glory of this quite small church is the magnificent arcade within. It has early stiff leaf or trumpet scallop capitals, and tongued waterholding bases of the early thirteenth century, coeval with the building of the castle by Sir Maurice (Berkeley) de Gaunt, co-founder in Bristol of St Mark's Hospital, whose church survives as the Lord Mayor's Chapel; he is also said to have been the founder of Bristol's Dominican Friary.[2] The interior is delightful: clear white walls, and atmosphere. The electric lighting is admirably and simply done from wrought-iron rings designed by John Roberts, and made by the Tetbury blacksmith. One of the Cotswolds' rare old rood screens survives; a squint-passage from chapel to chancel, and a Tudor stone pulpit. The roof is by Lewis Vulliamy, architect of Westonbirt House, *c.* 1844, a riot of ingenuity.

References

1 D. Talbot Rice, *English Art 871–1100*, page 96.
2 Bryan Little, Article on Beverston Castle in *Gloucestershire Countryside,* 1964.

WESTONBIRT

By 1858 the village had been pulled down and the cottagers rehoused away from the church, which was left in the garden of Mr R. S. Holford's new house now a school. To get to the church today we have to go through the village with cottages by Vulliamy, and past the golf-course, where, on an afternoon in term time, we will get a glimpse of the girls playing golf. We then walk along a sunken road through the fine specimen trees of the grounds, to the south entrance to the churchyard in front of the mansion. The tower is on the south and is Perpendicular, with battlements, gargoyles, a stair turret, and diagonal buttresses on the lower stage. The south porch has seats, and a niche on the east, all as we would expect for a village church; but inside it turns out to be a rather ordinary school chapel, packed with seats in the available space, and mostly rebuilt. There are a pair of sexless winged angels by R. Westmacott the younger of 1839, and a splendid recumbent effigy of R. S. Holford, 1892.

DIDMARTON WITH OLDBURY-ON-THE-HILL

This is a growing village on the main road near to the Worcester Lodge of Badminton. There are three churches if we count Oldbury-on-the-Hill. The church of St Lawrence is the medieval church of Didmarton, and because the Victorians chose to build a new church only about a hundred yards away, the old church is left very much as it must have been in the late eighteenth century, except that vandals and decay have done some harm. It is a most curious plan that exists now, with a nave and a north transept of almost equal size. The three-decker pulpit is very well sited for preaching in either direction, and is linked to the windows either side by a framing arch and pilasters. There is more Georgian furniture, but all of rustic quality. It is very much to be hoped that this little church will not now be lost to posterity.

Unfortunately the parish seems to prefer St Michael's, a dull church – even ugly on the north – by T. H. Wyatt, the Salisbury diocesan architect in 1872.

The church of St Arild at Oldbury is next to the Manor Farm and cannot be approached any other way except through the farmyard, and past this very pretty William and Mary house. Here again, as at St Lawrence, it is medieval with some Georgian box-pews and pulpit, untampered with except by time and decay. There is a surprise – a brand new stained glass west window, by Mr Crombie of John Hall's Studios in Bristol.

LEIGHTERTON

The church is in the middle of a compact little village with pretty cottage gardens in a sparsely inhabited part of the south Cotswolds.

In the churchyard there are table tombs. The tower has a nineteenth-century timber-framed belfry and the church has been much over-restored generally.

In the tower is a set of eight tubular bells, and two of orthodox type; one dated 1881, the other, dedicated to St George, cast at the Bristol foundry either late in the fifteenth century or early in the sixteenth.

BOXWELL

The church looks to be in a very private situation. It can only be approached by plunging through the box woods down the long drive of Boxwell Court, for here the plateau is beginning to break up into steep valleys. Church and house are almost joined, and the mown grass of the churchyard reveals a couple of grand table tombs.

The church is entirely delightful, even better inside than out, although there is a wonderful thirteenth-century bellcote, very massive, with an octagonal stone spirelet and grotesque corbels. Inside, the walls are lime-washed, and we are immediately struck by the Royal Arms of Queen Anne, 1702, over the tiny chancel arch and consequently filling quite a large space. There are also hatchments and monuments to the Huntley family who have lived in Boxwell Court since the Reformation. All is light for the windows have clear glass, and there are some old benches and Laudian communion rails. The three-bay north arcade is splendid in so small a church with octagonal piers of c. 1300, tall chamfered arches and a narrow aisle.

LASBOROUGH

Another hamlet on the banks near Boxwell, with, in this case, an entirely rebuilt church, by Lewis Vulliamy, 1861–62. On the other side of the valley stands the castellated mansion by James Wyatt. The church is in Decorated style, with a stone floor, lime-washed walls, light with clear glass, and an elaborate timber roof. The pews have roses in their finials, the communion rails are seventeenth century and the font Norman, in fact it is much duller outside than in; but it must be on the edge of redundancy.

NEWINGTON BAGPATH

The church is even more isolated and redundant than Lasborough, for there is no habitation close by, and it is now only approached by a grass lane, at the edge of a valley on one side, and huge high flat fields on the other. Apart from the chancel by S. S. Teulon, the church is unspoilt and unsophisticated, and the south doorway has a low, flat ogee-cusped arch reminiscent of Gloucester Cathedral ambulatory.

KINGSCOTE

The Perpendicular tower has a conspicuous stair turret with a spirelet, is of three stages and has battlements. Otherwise the church was much restored in 1851 by S. S. Teulon, and most of the windows are his, though a small lancet window survives on both sides of the chancel, giving totally inadequate light; in fact the church is extremely dark, and the north transept has been blocked off altogether and closed. There are several monuments to the ancient Kingscote family (which ends on the 1939-45 War Memorial) both inside, and outside in the romantic churchyard.

DURSLEY DISTRICT

Dursley, Uley, Owlpen, Nympsfield

DURSLEY

On the lower ledge of the escarpment, but not in the vale, Dursley church tower rises magnificently against the wooded banks beyond the town. It looks more like the vale towers of Gloucester and Thornbury than a Cotswold tower, as it has a pierced embattled parapet, and open pierced pinnacles. Of three stages, the second is panelled and has image niches which are supported on acanthus, thus indicating a date other than Perpendicular. Indeed it is a rebuild of 1709, and shows that Perpendicular Gothic survived into the period when it was revived.

A great part of the church is built of local tufa. Nothing appears earlier than the thirteenth century, and most of it is Perpendicular, or nineteenth-century work by Sir T. G. Jackson. The Perpendicular consists of a nave with arcades of ordinary octagonal columns, but with capitals enriched with carved flowers supporting extraordinary stilted arches, c. 1450. The eastern part of the arcade on the south has two bays with quite different mouldings to the rest, which open into what is still called Tanner's chapel, after a mid-fifteenth century merchant who endowed a chantry in the reign of Henry vi. However, the work looks as if it was not carried out till some time after his death. There is a cadaver effigy, supposedly of Thomas Tanner, of early sixteenth-century date. The porch *c.* 1480, has a parapet carved with quatrefoils and three image niches. Inside, the walls have grid panels, and there is a lierne vault with carved bosses, and a chamber above.

Looking at the church from outside the south porch, it has the real Perpendicular touch and the gargoyles fairly scream at us. Inside, the music comes from an organ in the choir, with a very good case made by Dr Arthur Hill in 1888.

ULEY

The church was rebuilt by S. S. Teulon in 1857–58, a few years before he did near-by Nympsfield. His tower is on the north and has three stages, with buttresses at right angles to the two lower stages. The upper stage has Decorated-style bell openings, an open parapet, and a small octagonal spirelet in one corner, crocketed, and with openings like a medieval chimney. It leaves only a confused picture in the mind. The unconventional windows with leaded lights like flowers and geometrical patterns are more memorable. The church it replaced seems to have been 'debased', and it was surrounded by out-door staircases leading to interior galleries.

The site is precipitous, with the churchyard falling away abruptly to the south, so that we are quite surprised to find the Rudder tombstone horizontal; but here he is, the father of the county historian. 'Underneath lie the remains of Roger Rutter, alias Rudder, who was buried August 30, 1771 aged 84, having never eaten Flesh, Fish nor Fowl during the course of his long life.'

It then says that he had one son, Samuel Rudder, born 21 December, 1726. This took place in the parish at Stout's Hill, before it was rebuilt in 1743, to the design of William Halfpenny, in delightful Gothick for a dashing young clothier called Gyde, whose own family tablet can be seen under the church tower.

OWLPEN

The church is situated on the bank just above and behind the romantic Tudor manor house. The view from the terrace on the south side overlooking the great manorial yews is one of deep enchantment; but the church is not old, in fact it has the most elaborate Victorian–Edwardian interior in the Cotswolds. The chancel has inlaid mosaics by Powell of Whitefriars Glass Works and an alabaster reredos, all of 1887. The floors are covered in encaustic tiles. At the other end there is a baptistry with mosaics also by Powell, but of the 1913 variety, with standard rose trees and lilies; even the stone jambs of the windows are inlaid with mother-of-pearl.

NYMPSFIELD

This is a satisfactory and suitable country church, typical of Teulon at his simplest, for it was built in 1861–63, by the famous Victorian architect, who was capable of far more extreme eccentricities than the peculiarly leaded windows here. The tower, however, is Perpendicular, and a pretty, tall example, with a stair turret very much in evidence, being higher than the battlements of the parapet. There are diagonal buttresses, and splendid gargoyles. The west doorway has a Tudor arch.

WOTTON-UNDER-EDGE DISTRICT

Wotton-under-Edge, North Nibley, Stinchcombe,
Ozleworth

As the name implies, Wotton is just under the edge of the Cotswold escarpment. It is a small town with a history, and quite a big church, east of which is the manor on the site of the Berkeleys' manor house. They lived there at times when excluded from Berkeley Castle. Katherine, Lady Berkeley, who founded the Grammar School in 1384, was the widow of Thomas, Lord Berkeley, who was accused of complicity in the murder of Edward II. Their grandson, Thomas, was buried in the church in 1417. At the end of the north aisle is his Purbeck marble tomb-chest, with his brass, and that of his wife, who died in 1392. The brasses are over 6 ft. long, and are said to date from then, so that they are some of the earliest and most beautiful in the Cotswolds.

This couple left only a daughter, Lady Warwick, thus causing the family's loss of succession which lasted for many years and caused the last private battle in England, at Nibley Green in 1470. By the time Leland visited Wotton *c.* 1530, the town was 'well occupied with clothiers'. Bigland states that Flemish weavers had come to

Wotton *c.* 1330; anyway by 1608 half the community was involved in the cloth trade, twice as many as were employed in agriculture.

The church has a fine Perpendicular tower at the west. It is of the Cotswold type rather than the Gloucester Vale or Somerset kind, and consequently has diagonal buttresses with string-courses running round them. The two top stages have crocketed pinnacles in relief on the buttresses, which terminate also in crocketed pinnacles above the embattled and panelled parapet. There are gargoyles, and two stages have panels with trefoiled heads in low relief, altogether pretty elaborate. The lower stage is earlier, and the west window even retains ballflower ornament which puts it back in the fourteenth century.

No part of the church is earlier than the thirteenth century, and this is the date of the arcades which divide the nave from the aisles, all three about 24 ft. wide and 90 ft. long, which gives a broad and open appearance. The chancel arch has gone. In the eighteenth century the nave roof was raised to allow for big clerestory windows, and *c.* 1800 the plaster ceilings were put in by the Nailsworth architect, Nathaniel Dyer, *c.* 1752–1833. This work was done for the vicar, the Reverend William Tattersall, who was astute enough to buy the St Martin-in-the-Fields' Organ, which had been presented by George 1 in 1726, built by Christopher Schrider, and played by Handel. In Tractarian times a choir was inserted where the chancel arch had been, and the existing low screen is rather unattractive. On the whole, however, there is a certain lightness and harmony about the interior. The tablets have been arranged on the walls more or less in symmetrical groups, and there are many of very good quality, reflecting the wealth and taste of the Georgian community in striking distance of Bath.

On the banks near Wotton-under-Edge are two churches, both medieval, and both much restored in the nineteenth century by the architect of Truro Cathedral, J. L. Pearson, though neither can be considered important works by his standards.

NORTH NIBLEY

The chancel was rebuilt by J. L. Pearson in 1861, with a complete scheme of interior decoration by Clayton & Bell. When it came to be restored by Mr Larkworthy in 1974 it was discovered that there had been a great deal of over-painting in about 1910, in some instances in colours which were not used by the Victorians. Only the east wall was largely unspoiled, together with the Clayton & Bell glass in the window. The vicar from 1859–81 must have been influenced by his Tractarian neighbours at Stinchcombe, but he only seems to be remembered for being married to Miss Purnell of Stancombe Park and is said to have created the garden in the valley, out of sight of his wife's house for private reasons.

On the wall of the south aisle there is an effigy of Grace Smyth, wife of the early seventeenth-century historian of the Berkeleys, John Smyth.

The belfry windows are filled with seventeenth-century (1632) stone tracery.

A ring of six bells, one of which was recast by Messrs. Warner, 1896; the others are by Abraham Rudhall 11, 1726.

STINCHCOMBE

The church was largely rebuilt by J. L. Pearson in 1855, not perhaps surprisingly since the Rev. Isaac Williams, the famous Tractarian, who wrote what was considered to be the very provocative Tract No. 80, in 'Tracts for the Times', on 'Reserve in communicating Religious Knowledge', was at the Vicarage from 1848 to his death in 1865, and Sir George Prevost, second baronet, a pupil and disciple of John Keble, was perpetual curate from 1834-93. The 'Bisley School' was the description given by Williams of himself, Prevost and Tom Keble. They were all deeply involved in the writing of the Tracts, though Prevost never wrote one, and were watching Newman to see if he went too far towards Popery.[1]

The chancel and sanctuary have seven steps, encaustic tiles, a carved and gilded reredos and furnishings by Pearson. The chancel windows are by Wailes, two in memory of Isaac Williams. The windows in the rest of the church are by Clayton & Bell, and are mostly very good. The only old parts kept were the north porch, and west tower though the spire may be Pearson's.

A ring of six bells; four by Messrs. Warner, late nineteenth century; two by the Whitechapel foundry, twentieth century.

References

1 Prevost correspondence. Record Office, Shire Hall, Gloucester.

OZLEWORTH

The church is really in the stable yard of the big house and has to be approached down the private drive. The churchyard is circular. Roger Berkeley gave the advowson to his Augustinian priory at Leonard Stanley before he died in 1131. There are several things about the church which are unusual, including the central hexagonal Norman tower which may have been the nave with an apse to the east and a narthex to the west. The west wall of the tower has an arch carved with deeply undercut and pierced chevrons; but before we get there we must enter by the south doorway, which is thirteenth century and has extraordinary and striking enrichment consisting of an arch with six big lobes or foils with stiff-leaf sprays in the centre of each and in the spandrels. Pilgrims arriving back at Bristol may have seen something like this abroad in France or Spain. The church was enlarged by the amateur architect and professional curate, W. H. Lowder, who spread a Victorian mantle including nasty shiny tiles, for not only did the people and servants from next door worship here, but also the gentry from Newark Park (now National Trust Property).

BISLEY DISTRICT

Bisley, Oakridge, Bussage, France Lynch

BISLEY

Here we come under the influence of Thomas Keble, Bisley's nineteenth-century vicar, whose powerful personality still over-powers everything for those who know about him. He was brother to John Keble, and was himself responsible for a Tract. He had a 'school' of Tractarian curates, and one of them, W. H. Lowder, was an amateur architect who restored Bisley Church as well as Miserden and Ozleworth. Keble was vicar from 1827 to 1873 and during that time undertook continuous building operations in the neighbourhood, giving valuable patronage to the young architect G. F. Bodley, who built the Bisley school just north-west of the church.

It was Keble or his son who invented the legend of the 'Bisley Boy' being substituted for Queen Elizabeth I when she was a girl, and bitterly he regretted it later when he realized people were really going to believe it. Another deception is connected with the font. Lowder's explanation is that in 1862 it was 'the work of an amateur carver whose happy ignorance of the art of modern stone carving has produced a spirited specimen of rude Anglo-Norman of the nineteenth century', and yet the Transactions of the Bristol & Gloucestershire Archaeological Society have reported it as taking a 'high place among Norman fonts'. There may be some truth, however, in the story that the people of Bisley were excommunicated for a couple of years some time before the Reformation, and had to bury their dead in Bibury churchyard, which was a peculiar and therefore outside the jurisdiction of the Bishop, and the nearest such, but even as the crow flies it would be quite a walk.

Tom Keble started with daily services in 1827, at that time unknown in the Church of England. Bisley church was one mass of private galleries, even one across the chancel arch. Mill-owners who had made money in Stroud came to live here, and erected their own staircases leading to their galleries. It is said there were 11 entrances, so there must have been stone stairs all round the building. All this was swept away by 1862, when the nave roof had to be rebuilt; the spire had been repaired in 1829, and the chancel restored in 1851.

The interior of the church is quite spacious with two tall arcades; but it looks somehow rather grey and untidy. The low Tractarian choir screen and other furnishings add to the clutter. In the vestry are some original wood carvings from the medieval roof.

A ring of eight bells; the five largest by Abel Rudhall 1747–1748; the others by John Warner and Sons, 1864.

The organ, rebuilt by J. W. Walker (1862), still needs a case.

OAKRIDGE

This is one of the churches built by Thomas Keble for the clothiers and mill-workers in 1837. It is on the edge of the built-up area on a sloping site, with a flat park-like field to the south before the big Frome valley. Close by is a 'Georgian-looking rectory' which enjoys the same view. Though built in ashlar, the church is plain 'Commissioner' type, broad and suitable for preaching; the interior is now enlivened by gay paintwork over almost everything. Just outside the south door are the graves of artists who recently lived in Oakridge, Sir William Rothenstein, who died in 1945, and William Simmonds, who died in 1968.

BUSSAGE

The village clings precariously to the top; but the church looks as if it has slid a good way down the side of the valley, a subsidiary valley to the Golden Valley. In fact it was built there in 1846 by J. P. Harrison, for Thomas Keble and a group of Oxford undergraduates who subscribed for the purpose. The south aisle was added by G. F. Bodley in 1854 when still under the influence of Sir G. G. Scott, and of course, Ruskin. It is therefore of interest to students of early Victorian and Tractarian church architecture.

One bell by C. and G. Mears, dated 1846.

FRANCE LYNCH

France Lynch and Chalford Hill are unlike other Cotswold places and resemble some parts of Yorkshire with their excessively steep and narrow lanes creeping between closely built mill-workers' cottages, on the side of the Golden Valley. The church was designed by the great Victorian church architect G. F. Bodley for Thomas Keble in 1855–57. It is one of his earliest works, and is in his French style with a dash of Ruskinism thrown in.[1]

References

1 David Verey, *Country Life*, May 20 1971. "Two churches by Bodley" (France Lynch and Selsley).

PAINSWICK DISTRICT

Painswick, Edge, Harescome, Pitchcombe

PAINSWICK

Famous for its churchyard, which must be about the best in England. Several of the table tombs have recently been restored with help from the Diocesan Table Tomb Fund, and Mr Denzil Young's *Tomb Trail* has been well researched, and can be bought in the church. The tombs were designed with the aid of pattern books in the tradition of the Renaissance and display baroque style, later rococo, like the plaster work in the house called The Beacon. Many are the work of the Bryan family. The tomb of John Bryan, Carver,

1787, is a stone pyramid, a model of Caius Cestius' tomb in Rome. He designed the north-east gateway to the churchyard, of which only the two outer pillars now remain, as well as many of the tombs. His clients were mostly clothiers. Others were yeomen, mercers, a gratuitous preacher, woolstaplers, a gentleman, a rector, a maltster, and Thomas Hamlett, a senior Free Mason who signs several brass plates. Probably the oldest is that of William Loveday, 1623. There are in all 73 historical tombs recorded on the excellent map of the churchyard in the Vicar's Vestry, where there is also John Bryan's Reredos, alas not used, with fluted Ionic columns and gilded sunrays. The yew trees were planted in 1792, and it is the combination of the clipped yews and the pedestals and table tombs which makes it so memorable.

After this, the church may perhaps be a disappointment, but the spire is most impressive. Again John Bryan is the hero, as it was he who rebuilt the top of the spire after it was struck by lightning in 1763. The north side of the church is better than the south because the south was rebuilt in the nineteenth century by Waller, who apparently destroyed a Georgian south aisle of 1741, which had a Doric arcade and must have gone far better with the churchyard and general feeling of Painswick. How ill-advised the Wallers often seem to have been. Mr Paterson's modern porch, however, goes very well considering the problems it has overcome. The north side has a Perpendicular aisle with a continuous parapet running into St Peter's Chapel, with gargoyles, pointed Perpendicular windows, and narrow buttresses. There is a Perpendicular west window also in the fifteenth-century tower, which has diagonal buttresses.

The total effect of the interior is very harmonious. The nave is exceptionally wide and the aisles comparatively narrow, so we have a good composition and good scale. A great deal of trouble has been taken with the decoration, particularly of the chancel and sanctuary roofs, and the colours are sympathetic. In the early twentieth century the vicar, William Herbert Seddon, provided a screen from Nuremberg; but this has now been moved to the Cathedral precincts in Gloucester, except for the part in the south aisle, and one small gate in the garden at the Cranham Woods Hotel, formerly called Gwynfa by Mr Seddon, who employed Temple Moore to build the big additions to the house, which included a chapel.

The organ, by John Snetzler, was introduced in 1814. The mahogany case is almost invisible.

EDGE

Samuel Whitfield Daukes was a typical, but above average early Victorian architect. One cannot study nineteenth-century architecture without coming across his name. His Romanesque church St Peter's Cheltenham is so remarkably out of the ordinary that no average ordinary architect could have done it.

He was born in 1811, and lived till 1880; but he never became a High Victorian. His style was eclectic. He was quite capable of designing in any style, according to the desires of his clients, or just as an exercise in versatility. He was Low Church by upbringing and remained so, though he admired the architecture of Pugin and was quite capable of pleasing a High Church client such as Father Lowder of St Saviour's Tetbury. In this case, in 1865, most of Daukes's chief works were completed and he had left Gloucestershire for London. The closest church is Falfield, which he designed five years earlier. After the consecration of Edge in June, Daukes said he had 'endeavoured to provide a church for the service of God, and suitable to the exposed position in which it was placed.'[1] It is rockfaced, and the windows have unmoulded architraves and plate tracery. Although small in scale, it is robust, with a turret on the more protected south side, quite simple with contrasting chamfered surfaces.

The need for a church here is said to have been because the corn merchant who built Harescombe Grange did not wish to walk across the fields to Harescombe church. The site of the new church was in fact closer to Horsepools, the residence of Samuel Bowly, a wellknown Quaker philanthropist. The newspaper report does not say who attended the consecration service, but only that the sum of £61 was collected.

References

1 *Wilts. & Glos. Standard*, 17 June, 1865.

HARESCOMBE

Harescombe may fairly be included as a Cotswold church though its neighbour Haresfield is not. Harescombe nestles at the foot of the escarpment. It is next the site of the medieval castle of the Bohuns, and overlooked by Haresfield Beacon, the property of the National

Trust. The churchyard has a very good collection of table tombs dating from 1671 to 1826, and they stand in what is, and should remain, a little conservation area full of wild daffodils in the Spring. The small church is notable for its thirteenth-century bellcote, which contains two bells, one of which is coeval with the church which was consecrated by the Bishop of Worcester in 1315. It has been described as of 'singular shape, long and tapering like the flower of the campanula.'[1] It is therefore, one of the oldest bells in the diocese, if not the very oldest. Its companion was recast in 1884. The bellcote is situated over the chancel arch, and has a small octagonal stone spire supported on two sides by walls, and on a stone bracket between the bells.

The church is delightful inside too, with an exceptionally good font of this early period, lime-washed walls, a proper 'English altar' with carved angels on riddel posts, and a painted country baroque monument to an eighteenth-century parson.

References

1 Transactions of the B. & G.A.S. Vol. X. 1885–86, page 105.

PITCHCOMBE

On a shoulder of the romantic hills between Stroud and Painswick, the church is a rather plain nineteenth-century rebuilding in pale grey ashlar, with a tower. The churchyard, however, has old table tombs by the Painswick masons.

CHIPPING CAMPDEN DISTRICT

Chipping Campden, Broad Campden, Ebrington, Saintbury,
Snowshill, Broadway, Blockley, Bourton-on-the-Hill

CHIPPING CAMPDEN

Apart from Cirencester, Chipping Campden and Northleach must be recognized as the two most splendid of the Cotswold 'wool' churches. Campden has a greatly more elaborate tower than North-leach; but it has not got anything like Northleach's magnificent porch. The two churches are, however, very alike in plan (see p. 34) and the treatment of their naves, arcades and clerestories are similar.

What wool merchants then were responsible for building Campden church?

First of all we know about Grevel, who has posthumously stolen the lime-light, perhaps because the inscription on his brass states that he was 'The flower of the wool merchants of all England.' He died in 1401, and his house survives in the town. He bequeathed one hundred marks 'to the new work to be carried on' in the church. Most of the important Perpendicular rebuilding however, was not done for another half century, and it seems most probable that Grevel's money went on work in the north aisle and north chapel where he was buried. His brass is not now *in situ*.

There were, however, other fifteenth-century wool-merchants in Campden like William Weoley (or Welley) who died in 1450, but whose will is not known. In 1440 he obtained 'letters of reprisals' from the King against the Florentines who owed him over £1,000 for wool, which indicates the vast extent of his business transactions. He is buried in the church, and his brass survives. He could obviously have left money for building. His family had been of considerable standing in Campden for many years prior to the fifteenth century. Not only was the town a trading centre for Cotswold wool, but by this time it had become the emporium for almost the whole of the wool produced in Wales.

About this time also there was a wool-merchant family called Bradway, a member of which, one John Bradway, was incumbent in 1460, and another, William Bradway, who died in 1488, left to 'the Bylding of the nave and body of the church one hundred marks', and a 'cheseble of white damask, with all the apparelle thereto belonging for a priest to sing masse'.[1] The Opus Anglicanum indeed of this date, and preserved in the church, is one of its greatest possessions.

To this William Bradway therefore, may be attributed the rebuilding of the nave arcades and clerestory, after 1488. One hundred marks is the same amount of money that Grevel left to the church (see p. 31), but Bradway specifically mentions the nave, and the problem for the masons was to insert it between the existing aisles and chancel, and to leave space for the building of the tower. The same problem had been faced at Northleach by John Fortey's mason. When Fortey died in 1458, work, we know from his will, was already in progress and continued afterwards, and work at Campden may have begun before 1488. At any rate 30 years is not too long in a mason's active life span to preclude his being the master mind of both churches, and in fact they must be by one and the same man. The nave arcade mouldings, bases, capitals and soffits are the same, as are the octagonal piers with exaggeratedly concave sides, producing the distinctive capital like a pagoda. The clerestory windows have different tracery to those at Northleach; but both are recessed with a deep hollow moulding on the inside, and rather near the surface on the exterior wall, with four-centred arched heads, and divided by strong vertical mouldings. There are east clerestory windows in both churches; both are structurally daring, though the tracery at Northleach is the more original and flowing, and can be seen more easily from the outside. The chancel here at Campden seems higher.

The tower came at the end of the Perpendicular rebuilding, and has the same look of calculated design and displayed virtuosity as the nave. Thin flat pilasters sweep up from the bottom culminating in ogee arches in front of the pierced parapet, an idea perhaps copied from Gloucester. One pilaster crosses the great west window so that it forms itself into a flying buttress springing from the point of the ogee arch of the deeply splayed west doorway. These are unforgettable features. The other sides of the lower stage are plain, and each stage gets gradually more elaborate till it is crowned with glorious crocketed pinnacles. The west window itself has mullions with roll mouldings, and five lights with ogee arches and a transom below which there is also tracery, with quatrefoils in circles, a late Perpendicular feature (cf. the east window at Fairford).

This culmination of Perpendicular architecture in the Cotswolds, to be found at Campden, provides by far the greatest interest; but there are other features that should perhaps be mentioned, in spite of the fact that of Norman remains there is hardly anything, except a corbel head. There are, however, such things as monuments. The south chapel has some fine monuments to the Earl of Gainsborough's family, including the recumbent effigies of Lord Campden and his wife *c.* 1629, and upright shrouded figures by Joshua Marshall, *c.* 1642. And there is the stained glass in the east window by Henry Payne, a member of the Birmingham school of artists, *c.* 1920; and, also medieval fragments in the tracery. The walls of the chancel are painted, and the walls of the rest of the church will look better when they are treated in the same way. It is a little unfortunate that the windows have diamond-shaped quarries because these do not suit Perpendicular windows.

A ring of eight bells: three dated 1678 from the Woodstock foundry; one dated 1683; one given in 1683 and recast in 1912; one recast by Abel Rudhall in 1737; and the remaining two were recast at the Foundry in the nineteenth century. Massive oak bellframe chiefly seventeenth century but containing portions of an earlier frame.

References

1 Percy C. Rushen, *History of Campden*, p. 25.

BROAD CAMPDEN

St Michael's Church was built by J. Prichard of Llandaff in 1868. C. R. Ashbee and the Guild of Handicrafts designed the communion rail in 1913.

EBRINGTON

This village is on the north-east outlyer of the Cotswolds and has an interesting church, interesting anyway for its curious contents. The small Perpendicular tower has diagonal buttresses on the west, the Norman south doorway is enriched with chevron moulding, there is a very good Perpendicular font, the nave looks spacious, the chancel is scraped. These are all features we have met time and time again in the Cotswolds; but after that is said, we have to admit that Ebrington Church takes a line of its own.

It is dedicated to St Eadburgha, a Saxon saint, patron of Pershore Abbey. The carving on the western capital of the south doorway is, according to Miss Brill, a manikin with outstretched arms. The door is fastened by an oak beam some six feet long; when not in use this mighty bolt slides into a hole in the wall. The porch is west of the south chapel, and there is a quatrefoil opening in its east wall so that persons in the porch can see the chapel altar. This chapel has a squint of its own to the High Altar, and a piscina.

At the back of the nave are texts on the wall giving St Paul's admonitions to husband and wives. The benchends appear to be fifteenth century; but we cannot linger here, and are drawn towards the chancel which has a very low east window filled with glass by Christopher Webb, 1964. On the north of the altar is a tomb chest bearing the coloured, larger-than-life effigy of Lord Chief Justice Fortescue, who died in the time of Edward IV; and on the opposite side of the chancel are the busts of a Keyte baronet and his wife, by

Thomas Burman, he with long untidy hair, 1662, contrasting with her neat head. There are several other monuments to the Keyte family, and their heraldry is everywhere; another tablet is by Eric Gill. The pulpit and sounding-board are dated 1697, and there is a board commemorating a bequest, in 1632, of the 'milk of ten good and sufficient milch kine to the poor from May 10th to Nov. 1st annually for ever'.

SAINTBURY

This church must be on the verge of redundancy. It is approached only by a foot-path about half-way up the escarpment edge over-looking a panoramic view into Worcestershire. The tower has a broach-spire so it can be seen for miles. Though inclined to be damp, it has a very cheerful interior well lit by a large Perpendicular window at the west (the tower is on the south) which is of grid pattern divided in the centre of a four-centred arch. It was almost taken over by the Campden Guild of Handicraft; C. R. Ashbee designed the wrought-iron chandelier in the chancel, and the Guild was responsible for the wagon roofs with their gilded bosses (before 1908), the north door with carved St Nicholas, the north chapel screen, altar ornaments, and rain-water heads. They left the delightful late eighteenth-century box-pews with their Gothick panels, and the beautiful Laudian communion rails, the ogee-shaped font cover and Jacobean altar, so the church retains many charming objects, even oil lamps.

SNOWSHILL

The church is a rebuilding, and comes as rather a shock in this beautiful hill village, situated in the most picturesque part of the Cotswolds. Designed by an unknown architect, it offends the eye with a tough tower and parapet unrelieved by any castellation, and hard plate-traceried windows. The interior is dull; but the font and pulpit are old, Perpendicular and Jacobean.

BROADWAY

The old church of Broadway, St Eadburgha's, is not in the village but some way along the road leading to Snowshill, and is therefore prettily situated in the tree-clad foothills of the escarpment. It should not be confused with St Michael's, a church of 1839 nearer to the village, and which has St Eadburgha's sumptuous Elizabethan pulpit, because the old church is not regularly used.

St Eadburgha's has a central tower and was Norman to its whole present length. The crossing is rather confused, with fourteenth-century arches having beautiful continuous chamfers; but there is plenty of space to see it, and as all clutter, like pews, has been removed, the bare matt-faced tiles of the floor come as a surprise.

The chancel retains its Laudian communion rails and bits of panelling. On the south wall is a tablet to Thomas Phillipps of Middle Hill, who made one of the greatest collections of books and manuscripts ever gathered together, one which is still appearing in the sale rooms to this day.

BLOCKLEY

This large church has features of all periods, even the most unexpected. The tower at first glance looks as if it might be Perpendicular; but a longer look shows that this is not so. It was in fact built in 1725, and is usually called Gothic survival, although the bell openings have quatrefoils which have the appearance of early Gothic revival. Furthermore, the buttresses are not set diagonally, the parapet pinnacles at the corners are square, and in the middle there are just crocketed finials, and the west window is blatantly Georgian. This beautiful golden-coloured tower was the work of Thomas Woodward, a mason architect of Chipping Campden.

Quite a lot of alteration had taken place a hundred years before in Laudian times, and the south porch is dated 1630.

However, many features are much earlier. The Bishop of Worcester had a residence here in the Middle Ages, and we know how peripatetic these bishops were. In 1270 the bishop made Blockley a prebend of his collegiate church at Westbury-on-Trym. The chancel is late Norman and had three bays prepared for vaulting. In the east angles are vaulting shafts, and there are other remains skilfully carved; but the walls are scraped and the effect spoilt.

The nave now has a flat plaster ceiling, and there are many eighteenth- and nineteenth-century monuments to the Rushout family of Northwick Park. In the churchyard a feature has been made of wrought-iron railings surrounding family graves.

A ring of eight bells; tenor by Mears, 1854; one by Abraham Rudhall 11, 1729; two by J. Taylor and Company, 1894; the remaining four by members of the Bagley family, 1638 (2), 1679 and 1683.

BOURTON-ON-THE-HILL

The name of this church is linked, or should be, with that of Dr Samuel Wilson Warneford, who was rector from 1810 to his death in 1855.[1] This clergyman gave away during his life the huge sum of £200,000, worth at today's values a vastly greater amount. It is to him that the Gloucester Diocese owes the Warneford Ecclesiastical Charity, and the Warneford Clerical Trust. His benefactions to Oxford and Leamington are well known. His sister Philadelphia died here in 1834, and his wife Margaret (née Loveden from Buscot Park) died in 1840. They were both as philanthropical as they were rich, particularly the sister who shared with her brother the many legacies that came their way. Their tomb is on the bank just west of the church tower.

In 1827, Dr Warneford re-pewed and galleried the church, put in an organ, and altered the place of the pulpit and font at his own expense, and without a faculty. Only one small part of the gallery has survived, just over the north-west corner of the north aisle.

The exterior of the church is attractive; of a good iron-stone colour, with a small Perpendicular embattled tower which has a higher stair turret, and diagonal buttresses on the west, Perpendicular clerestory, straight-headed Perpendicular windows, carved enrichment round the chancel parapet, and a Tudor south doorway with dragons carved in the spandrels.

The interior decoration shows a fashion which is the extreme opposite of scraping. Every detail has been uniformly lime-washed, even carved stone capitals and window tracery. This treatment obviously has its own successes and is very good for showing off stained-glass windows, if indeed they are worth looking at. Here the south arcade is Norman with round piers and scalloped capitals, and pointed Transitional arches. In the chancel there is a good 'English Altar' and organ case.

Of the ring of six bells the three largest are by Henry Bagley of Chacombe, 1677; one was recast by Mears and Stainbank, 1872; the others are by John Rudhall, 1792. In addition is a small sanctus bell, probably medieval.

References

1 E. G. C. Beckwith, *S. W. Warneford. LL. D.* 1974.

WINCHCOMBE DISTRICT

Winchcombe, Sudeley, Charlton Abbots, Hailes, Farmcote,
Didbrook, Stanway, Stanton, Buckland

WINCHCOMBE

The church is in the top category of Cotswold 'wool' churches, and is a complete rebuilding all of one date, so that there is no chancel arch or division between the nave and chancel. It is more economically built too, and is not so lofty as the naves of Northleach and Campden; but the continuous line of clerestory windows – all with straight heads like a long horizontal wall of glass – is most effective, specially as it continues into the chancel, although that is marked by a change in the tracery. The clerestory windows are in pairs of two lights each and they are very close together so the master mason was straining the construction to its utmost with considerable stress on the mullions. Above is an embattled parapet with pinnacles. The gargoyles have huge human heads and winged shoulders. The aisle windows have four-centred arches and the east window tracery is pretty. The west tower has diagonal buttresses, and the pinnacles are continued down to the top string-course, as in other Cotswold examples like Longborough. The porch is vaulted but is otherwise rather austere.

The interior is ashlar-faced. The arcades of eight bays have very flat four-centred arches, and there are no vertical features going up from the piers, as in most such churches, thus giving much emphasis to the horizontal line. In the chancel there is a sedilia which is contemporary, with elegant detail but little depth. This was built by the Abbot of Winchcombe Abbey for the townspeople who themselves paid for the rest. The reredos is Victorian and rather spoils the effect; the Puritan arrangement as seen in an old photograph looks better. Another photograph shows a west-facing gallery on top of the Perpendicular screen. These photographs are shown in the church with other 'museum' objects, like the splendid door from Winchcombe Abbey with the initials of the Abbot Richard Kidderminster 1488–1525, and a very flat four-centred arched head, a good example of late Perpendicular art.

The organ, of 1735, was enlarged 1890. It has a good case.

SUDELEY

Sudeley church is in the Castle garden and was built for Ralph Boteler (*c.* 1460) who also helped build Winchcombe church. The exterior of Sudeley Church is a very elegant piece of Perpendicular work, by the best masons going round in the peak period of Cotswold Perpendicular architecture. The west entrance (now made famous on TV in the Palliser plays) has a splendid window over, with carvings on the hood-mould, and an elegant bowtell between two hollow mouldings. Either side are nodding canopies over image niches (now filled with Victorian images). All round are flat buttresses which change to diagonal at the springing of the arches of the windows and continue up into pinnacles with large gargoyles on the string-course. The situation is perfect, with a view over the clipped yew hedges in the garden to the distant Cotswold hills. Inside all is Sir Gilbert Scott's creation, except for some early medieval glass. Queen Katherine Parr's effigy is by J. B. Philip, 1859, on a tomb chest designed by Scott.

CHARLTON ABBOTS

So called because it belonged to Winchcombe Abbey, and is where the monks had a leper hospital. It is certainly a remote and private place to this day, shared by the people in the manor, in the wooded hills on the edge of Sudeley Park. The church became ruinous in the eighteenth century and consequently looks over-restored, with shiny tiles on the floor and bare walls. It is very small and not without charm, however, with delightful rere-arches to the lancets in the chancel.

One fourteenth-century bell in open bellcote, probably from the Gloucester foundry.

HAILES

The small church was built *c.* 1130, before the great Cistercian Abbey which subsequently possessed it. The chancel is as broad as the nave and nearly as long. From the outside it looks nothing; but inside we surely gasp with pleasure, for here is a little unspoiled shrine, retaining features usually lost.

There are many tiles of the thirteenth century and later. The wall paintings of *c.* 1300 survive in the chancel, with shields of arms and heraldic devices including the eagle of the Earl of Cornwall who founded the abbey, and the castles of Eleanor of Castile. There are also fantastic animals and monsters. In the splays of the windows are two female saints; the one on the north is an exceptionally pretty girl and much clearer than most. In the nave also there are wall paintings;

a huge St Christopher on the north and a sporting scene on the south with lurcher dogs hunting a hare. There is also medieval stained glass. The fifteenth-century screen is *in situ* with part of a parclose as a western return on the south, indicating the existence of a small nave altar. All the furnishings are delightful and there is no clutter, also perhaps not much use.

FARMCOTE

This little church above Hailes has a most remote and beautiful setting with views towards the Malverns. It is also unspoiled. Remoteness has saved it; but can it now survive possible redundancy? Only the nave of the Norman church survives, with a Norman bell-cote partly built into the west wall. The door and windows on the south are Tudor; but the interior here is the best, with its fascinating collection of furnishings, pulpit and reading desk, Laudian communion rails, piscina with a wooden pillar, stone *mensa*, and recumbent effigies. The walls are lime-washed, and there are ledger stones on the floor.

DIDBROOK

In a very pretty situation on the foothills below the escarpment near Hailes, the church is said to have been rebuilt in *c*. 1475, by the abbot William Whitchurch.

The tower looks late Perpendicular with ashlar walls, diagonal buttresses, battlements, pinnacles, winged devil gargoyles, and a distinctly Tudor-looking west door and window. The tower is built into the nave, which is broad and aisleless. The interior is altogether delightful and unspoiled, with apparently no Victorian restorations. There are timber roofs, a Georgian chancel arch, seventeenth-century pulpit, and communion rails, a family box-pew, and fifteenth-century glass fragments.

The four bells by William Bagley, 1706, were melted down by J. Taylor and Company and cast into a ring of five in 1911.

STANWAY

The church is part of a group with the mansion and its famous seventeenth-century gatehouse; but it is inferior to these secular buildings owing to a far too thorough restoration in 1896. As we approach along its south side we pass the Norman chancel with its corbel table of grotesque heads which look as if they had mostly been recarved. The chancel south-west window is Perpendicular, with shaped stops to the hood-mould in the best tradition. The tower also is Perpendicular with battlements, and pinnacles on the corners; but no diagonal buttresses – only straight ones at the bottom. If we continue round the west end of the church and look back at the house, and if the sun is setting, every pane of glass in the great window of the hall will look like a bar of gold, clearly defined. And here too, we can see the raised ledger stone with lettering by Eric Gill, to the Countess of Wemyss, a great country-house hostess who died in 1937.

We must enter through the south porch where there is a bronze plaque by Alexander Fisher, who also made the St George on the War Memorial. Unfortunately the church has been scraped inside; but in the sanctuary the 'English Altar' is by Sir Ninian Comper, and Eric Gill did the lettering in the window splay on the north commemorating the men who fell in the Great War.

Four bells; two dated 1625 and 1638, by unidentified founders; one by John Rudhall, 1826; one by Messrs. Bond, 1904. Also a small sanctus bell, dated 1694.

STANTON

This village is usually considered, and probably quite rightly, to be the prettiest village in the Cotswolds. To be quite honest, it is not really on the top, but shelters immediately under the escarpment. It has the charm of perfection, and anything out of place would jar, but so far there isn't anything. The church adds to the enchantment, as it is also in its own way, perfect. The scale is quite small; but it has a spire which visually is a most useful adjunct.

It is approached from the south, and we immediately notice that the porch is treated as one with the south aisle and has a continuous Perpendicular moulded parapet with battlements and pinnacles. The Perpendicular windows are the grid variety, with two transoms in the upper half.

At first the interior seems medieval; but on second thoughts perhaps it is Sir Ninian Comper who has cast this subtly mystical spell. The pews are small enough to make the stone-flagged width of the central aisle tell. On the north the piers are late Norman and cylindrical, with stiff stalk capitals and water-holding bases with tongues; the south arcade is Perpendicular. There are transepts, both with piscinas, and both with east windows by Comper, that on the south having an altar and communion rails by Sebastian Comper. The great rood screen, western gallery, and alabaster reredos are all by Sir Ninian, and the east window was put together by him and contains fifteenth-century glass from Hailes Abbey. He signs his glass with a wild strawberry.

As at Evenlode, there is an early wooden pulpit, late fourteenth century perhaps. However, the one of 1684, with sounding board, is now used.

A ring of six bells; two by John Martin, of Worcester, 1659–60; the others by Humphrey and James Keene of Woodstock, 1640, a rare partnership.

BUCKLAND

The setting is immediately below the escarpment at its prettiest point below Snowshill, and separated from Broadway only by a knoll. The church stands on rising ground, and in the churchyard east of the chancel is the table-tomb of Colonel Granville. He died in 1725 and was the father of the famous Mrs Delany, who was the friend of Swift, invented 'flower mosaic', introduced Fanny Burney at Court, and in her autobiography makes one or two slight references to the village of her childhood. This period atmosphere almost survives inside the church (but not quite because Waller scraped it) for there are seventeenth- and eighteenth-century seatings, a western gallery, wainscoting with hat pegs, and wainscoting continuing round the east end indicating a Puritan arrangement of the Holy Table, though now there is a carved wooden Arts and Crafts reredos commemorating an officer killed in the First World War, and in the churchyard there are newer graves, including that of a Lady-in-Waiting to Queen Mary.

The east window has late fifteenth-century glass which represents three of the seven sacraments of the Catholic Church, Baptism and Confirmation together, Holy Matrimony and Extreme Unction. There is glass of the same period in the windows of the fifteenth-century hall in the rectory. William Morris paid for the glass in the church to be restored in *c.* 1883. Other treasures include a fifteenth-century blue velvet cope embroidered with pomegranates, together with portions of vestments from Hailes Abbey. Perhaps the strongest atmosphere is really pre-Reformation, for the Perpendicular architecture is there, with straight-headed windows in aisles and clerestory.

STOW-ON-THE-WOLD DISTRICT

Stow-on-the-Wold, Broadwell, Longborough, Condicote

STOW-ON-THE-WOLD

Quite a large church with projections in all directions, which rather destroy any feeling of unity. However, there is a splendid ashlar tower, Perpendicular of course, with an embattled and panelled parapet, with pinnacles and a string-course with gargoyles. It is placed on the south side, and opposite, on the north, is a transept. The church has a nave and aisles and is therefore quite broad. On the north is a porch which seems to be seventeenth-century Gothic, with huge yew trees almost growing into it, and Neo-Greek sarcophagi inside commemorating the Hippisleys who, with one short break, were rectors from 1744 to 1898.

The great west window is fine, with an ogee arch ending in a finial to contain an image, and with reticulated tracery of the fourteenth century. Other windows are earlier, and some Perpendicular ones have Tudor arches divided in the middle with a mullion.

The interior has an open south aisle with a vast picture by Gaspar de Craeyer, and the console of the organ which is in the north aisle. The floors are of stone. The main features of the cruciform plan were established before the end of the thirteenth century and the arcades were built about then. The church was restored by J. L. Pearson. As in Gloucester Cathedral, the west window has overpowering glass by Wailes, and here it is Wailes in the east window as well.

BROADWELL

The church is a little distance from the village, much nearer to the manor house, and not far from Stow-on-the-Wold. The churchyard has a collection of table tombs. Inside, the church is lime-washed, and has a very good arcade on the south with four bays of cylindrical piers and moulded capitals of thirteenth-century date. The south aisle has remains of its chapel in the canopied piscina. The floors are generally of stone. In the chancel the roof is painted, and so is the organ case, and there is a string-course; but the Ward & Hughes east window is not so good. Generally in this church the interior is better than the outside, though there is a beautiful Norman tympanum carved with a Maltese Cross, rebuilt into the exterior stair-case of the tower.

In the tower is a sanctus bell by Edward Neale, 1672; and a ring of five, one of which was cast at the Aldbourne, Wiltshire, foundry, another by Thomas Rudhall, 1761, and the remainder by the Bonds of Burford.

LONGBOROUGH

A large village with a large church. The top of the Perpendicular west tower resembles the one at Oddington old church, with central pinnacles continuing down to string course level, and corner ones starting from the top of the embattled parapet; and there are gargoyles. The lower stages are earlier. However, as we approach we are most struck by the marvellous south transept which is fourteenth century and has a south wall almost entirely composed of glass, supported by the prettiest buttresses at the sides and east and west. It has battlements and gargoyles, and reticulated tracery. The north transept is a very different thing, as it is the private pew designed by C. R. Cockerell in 1822 for Sezincote.

We enter through the Norman south doorway and find the interior is dark with scraped walls and awful glass of 1894 by Ward & Hughes. Again we find the south transept the most interesting part, although the fact that there is no way in to the Sezincote pew (or gallery as it appears) from the body of the church is intriguing. The south transept – or is it a chantry chapel? – is well lit. Below the window there lies the effigy of a knight, whose head is supported by beautiful winged angels of fourteenth-century date, on a tomb chest which has an ogee arcade with crocketed pinnacles. Is it his chantry? The well-preserved reredos on the east wall is *en suite* with the castellated sills of the windows. There are fragments of medieval glass in the west window tracery. Also, crammed into the south side of the transept is another noble tomb, that of William Leigh, and his wife, widowed for 34 years, who died in 1665 aged 83, and of whom it is reported 'She gave refuge to the faithful followers of the King'.

Two of the ring of six bells are by Richard Keene of Woodstock, 1680; one by Abel Rudhall, 1739 and the remainder by Messrs. Bond, 1898.

The organ, by Nicholson & Co., is of 1867.

CONDICOTE

The church is situated on the edge of an enclosed village green with farms all round. It is of archaeological interest, and has some interesting Norman features; but it underwent a too vigorous restoration when the interior was scraped in 1888.

The chancel is Early English and has buttresses; there is a window with plate tracery and a lowside window, and there are two-headed corbels at the eaves corners at the east. The Norman south doorway is very good, and has unusually enriched jamb shafts with twisted bead mouldings continuing round the roll moulding of the arch. On the south there is a good Perpendicular window with grid tracery, and a pedestal for an image inside, against its hollow moulded eastern jamb. This arrangement is similar to one at Upper Swell. The pointed chancel arch has chevron mouldings. The floor is stone with ledger stones. The chancel retains its string-course and piscina.

ANDOVERSFORD DISTRICT

Whittington, Dowdeswell, Shipton Oliffe, Shipton Sollers, Sevenhampton, Hawling, Salperton, Hazleton, Compton Abdale, Notgrove, Aston Blank, Turkdean, Clapton

WHITTINGTON

On the opposite side of the road is the beautiful park of Sandywell, with its very early eighteenth-century house (wings added after 1758). The church is almost touching Whittington Court at its west end, and it is usually entered by a door at the east end. The plan is curious as the west end of the nave has a narrow south aisle, and a two-bay arcade, one arch of which is restored Norman, the other Perpendicular with human head stops of the fifteenth century. There is a wider south aisle farther east, on the floor of which are three good fourteenth-century effigies rather casually placed, two knights and a lady. There is also a brass dating from the reign of 'King Philip and Queen Mary'. Most of the windows are Tudor.

DOWDESWELL

Situated above Cheltenham, commanding very fine views, and next a group of Jacobean houses, the church has a central tower with a small spire. The crossing is vaulted and is fourteenth century, but the spire was rebuilt in 1577. The Norman tympanum with the Tree of Life motif is set up, obviously not *in situ*, in the gable end of the south organ chamber. The interior though small is impressive because the chancel floor is stepped up very high over a vault. Two galleries with outside doors and private staircases survive here; this is unusual as in most places the galleries and private staircases were swept away. There are some good monuments and hatchments to the Coxwell-Rogers family and the brass of a priest, *c.* 1520.

SHIPTON OLIFFE

Macadamized churchyard paths lead to a door on the south, past the west end which is about the best part of the church with a very fine bellcote. This is thirteenth century with a pyramidal roof supported by pinnacled buttresses, and a central pilaster buttress running up the wall. The rest of the building is generally thirteenth century, with an Early English chancel and south transept, or chapel. The walls are lime-washed and there are black letter Commandments.

SHIPTON SOLLERS

A very small church with straight-headed Perpendicular windows with tracery on the south, though the fabric is thirteenth century. It was not restored till 1929, and so the pulpit and sounding board survive, and appropriate glass was added by Geoffrey Webb, and a reredos by Ellery Anderson, giving the church a shrine-like quality.

SEVENHAMPTON

Alec Clifton-Taylor[1] says of Sevenhampton: 'the church stands in a yard so well planted and so beautifully kept that the maintenance, one feels, must be almost a full-time job in itself. Time and skill could hardly be expected to give greater pleasure.' This is true, although as a general rule I think it is better not to try to garden in churchyards; but here we have a happy sensation approaching the church between borders of lavender and roses, and noticing the table tombs among the flowering shrubs, because it is so well done. The church itself looks entrancing with its central tower dividing the roofs of nave and chancel which are exactly the same height, a most unusual feature, and beautifully clad in Cotswold stone slates. As we arrive at the south porch we see that it has a late Perpendicular entrance with a flat arch, pierced quatrefoils in the spandrels, a straight head and stops carved with roses. The tower is elegant in that the mouldings on the string-course and parapet are refined, and this we can see as we look up; but the real surprise is inside where it transpires that it is a lantern tower over a crossing, ingeniously inserted *c.* 1500, with a lovely little tierceron vault, well lit by four-centred arched windows with blue and clear glass. This was the gift of a wool merchant called John Camber whose brass also survives.

A ring of three bells; one from the Gloucester foundry, late fifteenth century; another dated 1650, probably by John Pennington; the tenor by Abraham Rudhall (it could be A.R. 1 or Abraham 11) 1718.

References

1 A. Clifton-Taylor, *English Parish Churches as Works of Art*. Batsford, 1974.

HAWLING

In very countrified surroundings approached by a gated road through rolling wooded wolds from Guiting Power, the church sits close to the manor house. It has an exceptionally rich Perpendicular tower, perhaps again the gift of a wool merchant of significance. The tower is faced in ashlar, and has not got diagonal buttresses; but buttressing is at right angles in the lower stage with clasping pilasters above, over which runs a continuous string-course. There are battlements, pinnacles, gargoyles, and ogee-headed bell openings, all on a small elegant scale, the thoughts of a master mason in stone, far smarter than the ordinary small church Perpendicular tower.

The rest of the church was altered in Georgian times and never put back as was usual in later Victorian days, so we have a Venetian window in the east end with clear glass, so clear that it causes a glare in the eyes of the congregation. Unfortunately the Victorians did manage to insert shiny tiles on the floor, which mars what could be a pure Georgian atmosphere. The churchyard has some good headstones and table tombs, on one of which is a copper plate dated 1693, which looks as if it was put up yesterday. Some people are of the opinion that churchyards should be left fairly wild so that wild flowers can grow in them, which otherwise might disappear owing to the exigencies of modern farming.

SALPERTON

In order to get to the church we have to walk along the parterre immediately in front of the windows of the mansion, from where there is a most romantic view of the park. This was very civilized and eighteenth century and not typical of the high wolds, but now it is a little forlorn.

The church has a Perpendicular tower with battlements, gargoyles and diagonal buttresses. As we approach the north porch we pass some Renaissance table-tombs. The porch has seats and a small image niche on its east wall.

Inside the church we should notice the wall painting on the north side of the Perpendicular tower arch depicting a larger-than-death skeleton; otherwise the walls are lime-washed. There are two late Perpendicular windows on the south with straight heads, and glass by Walter Tower.

A static chime of three bells by Gillett and Johnston, 1952.

HAZLETON (OR HASELTON)

This is an extremely countrified place, high up in rolling hills. The church stands well among the farmyards, with a pleasant little churchyard containing an unusual number of very early table tombs, including one with perhaps a thirteenth-century incised cross, another enriched with possibly sixteenth-century Tudor roses, and a huge stone coffin just by the doorway.

The small west tower is Perpendicular, with battlements, diagonal buttresses, Tudor arched bell openings, and bold plinth moulding. The south porch has heavy buttresses, a niche on the east wall, and a Norman south doorway with chevrons at right angles. The interior of the church is not so good. A north aisle was added in 1866 by James Medland, who was expert in Neo-Norman elsewhere. One of his windows now has unsatisfactory modern Hardman glass. The floor is tiled. The walls, however, are lime-washed and there are Perpendicular windows in the chancel.

In the tower are two bells; the larger by Abraham Rudhall 11, 1721, the saunce by Thomas Mears, 1840.

COMPTON ABDALE

The church was a possession of the Priory of St Oswald in Gloucester, which was founded in 909, when Queen Ethelfleda brought there the body of St Oswald, king and martyr. It may seem surprising that no Norman features remain; but subsidence has evidently been a problem from the start on the sloping site. The church, dedicated to St Oswald, is really a rebuilding in Perpendicular times, and it can be considered as a 'wool' church.

Mrs Katharina Kosmala has kindly pointed out to me that St Oswald's Priory devolved its rectorial responsibilities on their tenant farmer, including the care of the chancel and the payment of the curate. In view of the poverty of the Priory and the wealth of the Rectory farmer and others in the village, it seems that the Priory had very little to do with the enlargement of the church and the building of the magnificent tower in the fifteenth century. The *couchant* animals on the buttress offsets of the tower are Cotswold rams, a sure sign that the money came from wool. Compton Abdale had through the wool trade close connections with Northleach, not many miles distant. It is also near Withington and Chedworth, both of which had great Perpendicular additions.

Can any resemblance between it and Northleach be detected? The Perpendicular windows at Compton Abdale consist of the east window and two windows in the north aisle, all of which have embattled transoms in the tracery, and this is a feature to be found at Northleach, combined with a central ogee-headed light. The other Perpendicular windows are in the tower, which has belfry louvres of two lights with ogee heads, and a very nice west window of three lights, the central one ogee-headed, with a great hollow moulding, and a hood-mould with curly stops surmounted by the head of a man blowing a horn, which is evidently a representation of St Oswald, the horn being one of his four emblems. Finally, the south wall of the nave has one straight-headed Perpendicular window with a pronounced hollow moulding outside containing centrally the head of the 'green man' or 'jack-in-the-green' with foliage growing out of his mouth. The other windows in this wall are nineteenth-century copies put in by the Rev. Henry Morgan in 1881 to replace 'two very unsightly windows'.

The north arcade has octagonal piers with straight chamfers. If these had been hollowed as at Northleach and Chipping Campden, there would be the sought-after similarity; but they are not, perhaps simply because there was not that kind of money here. The tower, however, is elaborate by any standards. It has very beautiful battlements moulded and chamfered, with pinnacles at the four corners consisting of castellated turrets surmounted by unidentified heraldic animals. Are they Warwick bears holding ragged staves? The Warwick family owned Chedworth. Or are they the dogs or wolves of the Howe family of near-by Compton Cassey? The small sculpture set into the gable of the north porch is very weathered but still recognizable as a crowned head, and so perhaps another image of St Oswald.

A fragment of wall-painting came to light in 1965 and was treated and preserved by Mrs Eve Baker. It is part of a seventeenth-century cartouche, a satyr-like head with a large crown above it. There are more paintings under the lime-wash of this south wall; at least three layers with a very good range of colours, including reds, ochres, greens and blacks, and Mrs Baker thinks they should be uncovered.

The glass in the east window is by Hardman of Birmingham *c.* 1896. The furnishings in the chancel date from the restoration of F. W. Waller in *c.* 1904.

The four ancient bells were melted down in 1880 by Messrs. Warner and cast into a ring of six.

NOTGROVE

The small church is almost in the grounds of the Manor House. As we approach from the north-east we pass a collection of tombstones thrown down flat on the ground under an enormous yew tree, which is certainly one way of dealing with the mowing problem. We must now pass round the east end, and here we notice an external niche into which is inserted a crude Crucifixion, possibly Saxon. The south porch is in front of the manor. Here we can see the Decorated tower with its little octagonal spire. The nave windows on this side are restored straight-headed Perpendicular. Inside the porch there is a deep niche on the east, with an ogee head, the late Perpendicular feature so common in Cotswold porches.

We enter, and facing us there is a Norman arcade and narrow north aisle; the round piers have large overhanging scalloped capitals like those at Farmington and elsewhere on the Cotswolds. Unfortunately the walls are scraped. The church was restored by a nineteenth-century architect called J. E. K. Cutts, who supposedly scraped Temple Guiting also.

The east wall of the chancel is a blank like it is at Aston Blank. The fourteenth-century reredos is covered by a modern tapestry which echoes its original architectural form, and was finished in 1954. The floor of the choir is a pleasant mixture of stone flags and tiles. Either side are Whittington monuments; on the south two gentlemen, one above the other, which reminds us of Swinbrook, rather stiff fifteenth-century effigies, with plenty of Renaissance strap-work above; on the north in the sanctuary, a seventeenth-century lady's effigy, and two Caroline chairs. In the north transept there are also two fourteenth-century priests' effigies.

Other features of interest are the Norman tub-shaped font with a double band of cable-moulding beneath the rim, and the woodwork generally. There are several old benches, a screen, and a panelled pulpit. In the vestry is a stained-glass Virgin, *c.* 1300.

A ring of three bells; the treble with an unintelligible inscription, probably dating from the Reformation period; the second by John of Gloucester *c.* 1350; the tenor by Thomas Rudhall, 1770.

ASTON BLANK

This small upland church has a very good Perpendicular west tower of three stages with straight buttresses which change at a set-off at belfry level into diagonal. The buttresses are crowned with pinnacles with pretty little ogee gables, and the parapet has battlements and gargoyles on a string-course. Under the tower is a stone tierceron-vault with winged angels and corbels. The west window is also distinguished and the crowning part of the tracery is influenced by the east window in Northleach chancel. The Perpendicular windows on north and south have straight heads over three traceried ogee lights. All is evidently the work of the best Cotswold masons, and is the fifteenth-century aggrandizement of a Norman church, which appears never to have had an east window. Instead there are the remains of an elaborate fourteenth-century reredos, and on the north wall an Easter Sepulchre in the same style, heavily canopied and with a deep recess. A few Norman carved stones are preserved in an archaeological way in the porch.

A ring of five bells; one by J. Taylor and Company, 1880; another by John Rudhall, 1796; remainder by Abraham Rudhall 1, 1717.

TURKDEAN

Another church near Northleach which shows Northleach details having been copied. The two arched Perpendicular windows on the south side of the aisle have crowning tracery similar to that in the great east window of Northleach chancel. On the north the Perpendicular windows have straight heads with dripmoulds having deep drops with stops surrounded by bowtell moulding. They have two lights and have neat ogee mouldings on surrounds and mullions. The north doorway is also an accomplished piece of Perpendicular masonry with carved spandrels and pretty male and female stops to the label. Inside the church there is a Perpendicular arcade on the south. The west exterior wall preserves Norman carved stones and typical flat Norman buttresses. The interior of the church now presents a pleasing appearance; the chancel is nicely furnished for congregational use, and the nave is left almost empty, with faded wall-painting on the walls, and a simple naturalistically painted screen (1949, by Peter Falconer) dividing one from the other.

A saunce by Edward Neale, 1663, is preserved in the chancel, and three bells in the tower to which at the moment we cannot gain access; one is seen from below to be a fourteenth-century casting; another by E. Neale, 1641, has fallen on to the second floor.

CLAPTON

A tiny church on the edge of very high-up wolds. It has a large stone roof and stone-clad turret containing one small bell by Henry Bagley, 1742. There is a small Norman east window, and most of its fabric is late Norman. The church is chiefly known for the inscription on the north respond of the chancel arch which is an indulgence of a thousands days for the devout rendering of a *Pater et Ave* three times. Well worth it, one would think.

INDEX

Numbers in italics refer to illustrations.